Copyright © 2025 Michael Szymczyk

All rights reserved. No part of this book may be used, reproduced or trans from the author, except for citations and quotations with attribution or non-profit usage. For other uses, please request permission at info@vidart.org.

Szymczyk, Michael, 1981-
The Ultimate Wedding Planning Guide: Everything Engaged Couples Need to Know
ISBN: 9798308664093

The Ultimate Wedding Planning Guide: *Everything Engaged Couples Need to Know*

CONTENT

Introduction: Welcome to Wedding Planning

- A warm introduction to the book and its purpose.
- Encouragement for couples starting their journey.
- A brief overview of what the book will cover.

Part 1: Laying the Foundation

1. Setting Your Budget
    - Understanding costs and how to allocate funds.
    - Tips for saving money without sacrificing quality.
2. Choosing the Date
    - Seasonal considerations, availability, and significance of dates.
3. Finding the Venue
    - Factors to consider: location, size, theme, indoor/outdoor options.
    - Venue checklist and questions to ask during tours.
4. Building Your Guest List
    - Deciding who to invite and managing RSVPs.
    - Navigating tricky guest list politics.

Part 2: Creating the Look and Feel

1. Crafting Invitations and Save-the-Dates
    - Selecting designs, paper types, and wording.
    - Timing for sending invitations and tracking RSVPs.
2. Dreaming Up Your Decor
    - Inspiration for themes, colors, and personalized touches.
    - Working with florists and rental companies.
3. Finding the Perfect Dress (and Attire for Everyone Else)
    - A guide to bridal dress shopping and alterations.
    - Options for the wedding party and guest dress codes.
4. Floral and Decor Arrangements
    - Selecting flowers that fit your theme, season, and budget.
    - Tips on DIY vs. working with a florist.

Part 3: Assembling Your Dream Team

1. Photography and Videography
    - What to look for in a photographer/videographer.
    - Must-have shots and video moments to discuss in advance.
2. Hiring Vendors
    - How to choose caterers, bakers, DJs/bands, and officiants.
    - Contracts, communication, and managing expectations.

Part 4: Bringing it All Together

1. Planning the Ceremony
    - Designing the flow: vows, rituals, music, and traditions.
    - Tips for working with officiants and including personal touches.
2. Organizing the Reception
    - Setting the schedule: meals, speeches, dances, and entertainment.
    - Ideas for activities and surprises that guests will love.
3. Creating a Day-of Timeline
    - Sample schedules for smooth transitions.
    - Handling last-minute emergencies.

Part 5: Pre- and Post-Wedding Essentials

1. Pre-Wedding Events
    - Planning engagement parties, bridal showers, and bachelor/bachelorette parties.
    - Rehearsal dinner tips and etiquette.
2. Travel and Accommodations
    - Ensuring guest comfort with lodging and transportation.
    - Managing your own travel plans for the honeymoon.
3. Post-Wedding Checklist
    - Writing thank-you notes and handling gifts.
    - Preserving your dress and reliving memories through photos/videos.

Conclusion: Enjoy Your Special Day

- Encouragement to relax and cherish the big day.
- Tips for staying present and enjoying the moment.

Additional Resources

- Sample budgets, timelines, and checklists.
- Links to wedding planning apps and websites.
- DIY wedding photography, videography, catering, DJ and more.
- Sample playlists for the music
- List of wedding poses for stylized wedding portraits.
- More tips to look your best in wedding photos.

Introduction

Congratulations! Whether you've just said "yes" or have been dreaming of your wedding day for years, you're about to embark on one of the most exciting journeys of your life. Planning a wedding is no small task, but with a little organization, creativity, and guidance, it can be one of the most rewarding experiences you'll ever have. This book is here to help you navigate every step of the way. I've tried to make this book a short, concise guide you can read in less than a day, but with some helpful tips you won't find in other books that are based on my personal experiences having worked thousands of weddings.

A wedding is much more than just a single day—it's a celebration of love, commitment, and the beginning of a new chapter in your life. While the thought of planning such an important event might feel overwhelming at first, rest assured that it's also an opportunity to express your personality, style, and the unique story of your relationship. Every choice you make—from the venue to the music to the smallest decor details—can reflect who you are as a couple.

This guide is designed to take the stress out of wedding planning and replace it with excitement and confidence. Whether you're planning a grand event with hundreds of guests or an intimate ceremony with just a few close friends and family, this book will provide you with practical advice, step-by-step instructions, and plenty of inspiration.

Here's what you can expect as we go through this journey together:

1. **Laying the Foundation:** We'll start with the big picture, like setting your budget, choosing a date, and finding your dream venue.
2. **Creating the Look and Feel:** Next, we'll dive into the fun part: designing your invitations, picking your decor, and finding the perfect dress.
3. **Assembling Your Dream Team:** You'll learn how to select the right vendors—photographers, caterers, DJs, and more—to make your vision come to life.
4. **Bringing it All Together:** From crafting a day-of timeline to organizing your ceremony and reception, we'll ensure everything flows smoothly.
5. **Pre- and Post-Wedding Essentials:** Finally, we'll cover the finishing touches, like planning pre-wedding events, writing thank-you notes, and preserving your memories.

Throughout this book, you'll find checklists, tips, and real-world advice to make the process easier. Remember, there's no "one-size-fits-all" wedding. Whether you're following traditions or creating your own, your wedding should reflect your unique love story.

About Me
I'm an independent filmmaker that has started and built-up several small businesses, some which were successful, and some which failed, and when I'm not busy creating movies (fun fact: you can spot me drinking a fake Budweiser next to Jason Statham in *Wildcard*) or working on a startup, I learn foreign languages, write

books, and work as a professional wedding photographer and videographer. Why? Because it's what I love to do. For nearly two decades now, I've had the honor of helping couples capture one of the most important days of their lives.

I've seen it all—weddings with hundreds of thousands of dollars spent, featuring thousands of guests, and then the next day, I might be capturing a shotgun courthouse ceremony in the dead of winter, followed by an intimate reception at a local coffee shop with just a few family members and friends. This book is designed with all budgets in mind because no matter how extravagant or simple, the most important part of a wedding is the commitment you're making to your partner.

You're about to take one of the biggest steps in your life's journey—perhaps one that leads to building a family as special as the one you grew up in. Like a wedding, it is going to be full of joy, but it'll also take some work to pull it off!

So, take a deep breath, and let's get started. With a bit of planning and a lot of heart, your wedding day will be everything you've dreamed of and more.

Part 1: Setting Your Budget

Before you go into planning the details of your wedding, one important step will serve as the foundation for everything else: *setting your budget*. While it may not be the most glamorous part of wedding planning, establishing a clear financial framework will save you from stress and surprises down the road. This chapter will guide you through creating a realistic budget that matches your vision and priorities.

Step 1: Start with a Total Budget

Decide on the total amount you and your partner are comfortable spending. Consider these factors:

- *Who's contributing?* Have open conversations with family members if they've expressed interest in helping financially.
- Avoid starting your married life burdened by unnecessary debt—plan for a wedding that aligns with your financial comfort zone. Even if you have the funds available, ask yourself: *Do I really need to spend it all?* A lavish wedding might impress others, but it's not worth sacrificing your future financial stability. Consider the bigger picture: Will overspending now mean delaying a down payment on your first home? Will it leave you without a safety net if one of you faces unexpected job loss? What truly matters is the commitment you're making to each other. Don't let salespeople or vendors pressure you into spending more than necessary. Having worked in the wedding industry, I've seen how unethical practices can manipulate couples into purchasing unnecessary extras that end up costing thousands of dollars. While it's nice to have certain luxuries, remember that wedding expenses can spiral out of control if you're not careful. Stay focused on what's meaningful to you, and don't be afraid to say no to anything that doesn't add genuine value to your day. Now, on the other hand, if your parents are footing the bill, *I know a really good photographer*. Just kidding, but seriously, even when someone else is paying, focus on the essentials like the dresses, the venue, the food or catering, and don't get carried away.
- Be flexible. Leave some wiggle room for unexpected costs (aim for 5-10% of your total budget).

Step 2: Prioritize What Matters Most

Every couple has different priorities. Sit down together and decide what's most important to you. For example:

- Is the venue the crown jewel of your day?
- Do you want to splurge on photography and videography to preserve your memories?
- Are you dreaming of a gourmet menu and signature cocktails?

Rank your top three priorities as a couple. This will help you allocate your budget more effectively.

Step 3: Understand the Breakdown

Here's a general guide to how wedding budgets are typically divided. Adjust these percentages to fit your priorities:

- Venue and Catering: 40-50%
- Photography/Videography: 10-15%
- Attire: 8-10%
- Decor and Flowers: 8-10%
- Music and Entertainment: 8-10%
- Stationery (Invitations, Save-the-Dates): 2-3%
- Favors and Miscellaneous: 2-3%
- Planner/Coordinator (if hired): 10-15%

Step 4: Track Your Spending

Use a wedding budget spreadsheet, app, or planner to keep track of every expense. Here's what to include:

- Deposits and due dates for vendors.
- Payment milestones for services.
- Estimated vs. actual costs to help you stay on target.

Step 5: Plan for Hidden Costs

Wedding budgets often go over because of unforeseen expenses. Watch out for these commonly overlooked costs:

- Service charges and gratuities for vendors.
- Postage for invitations and thank-you notes.
- Alterations for attire.
- Overtime fees for venues, DJs, or photographers.
- Transportation for guests or wedding parties.
- Taxes and fees not included in quotes.

Step 6: Create a Savings Plan

If your wedding date is a year or more away, set up a savings plan to help fund your budget. Break it down:

- How much do you need to save monthly to meet your goal?
- Open a dedicated wedding savings account to avoid mixing funds.

Final Tip: Stay True to Yourself

Your wedding budget is personal. Don't feel pressured to overspend or match someone else's event. The most memorable weddings are those that reflect the couple's unique love story—not the size of the price tag.

Tips for Saving Money Without Sacrificing Quality

Your wedding doesn't need to break the bank to be beautiful, memorable, and uniquely yours. With a little creativity and flexibility, you can cut costs without cutting corners. Here are some tried-and-true ways to save money while keeping the quality of your big day intact:

1. Pick an Off-Peak Date

- Save on venue costs by choosing a weekday or an off-season date (late winter or early spring). Venues and vendors often offer discounts during less popular times.
- A morning or afternoon wedding can also reduce catering and venue fees.

2. Simplify Your Guest List

- Reducing your guest count is one of the most effective ways to lower costs, from catering and seating to invitations and favors.
- Focus on inviting close family and friends who are truly part of your journey.

3. Use Non-Traditional Venues

- Consider parks, libraries, backyards, or community halls instead of high-end wedding venues.
- Outdoor weddings can provide stunning backdrops with minimal decor costs.

4. DIY Where It Counts

- Handcraft elements like invitations, table centerpieces, or party favors to save money.
- Be realistic: DIY is great for manageable projects but avoid overcommitting to labor-intensive tasks.

5. Rethink Catering Options

- Opt for buffet-style meals, food stations, or brunch menus instead of formal plated dinners.
- Consider using a local restaurant or food truck instead of traditional caterers.
- Reduce costs by serving signature cocktails and wine instead of a full open bar.

6. Rent Instead of Buy

- Save money by renting decor, tableware, and even wedding attire.
- For your wedding dress, check out consignment shops or rental services for designer options at a fraction of the cost.

7. Photography and Videography

- Hire Professionals with Packages That Match Your Budget: When it comes to DJs, photography and videography, finding a professional whose services fit your budget can be challenging. Many wedding photographers and videographers charge high fees—and for good reason. Their work often involves hundreds of hours of work, from pre-wedding consultations and planning to editing and post-production, not to mention the skill and precision required on the wedding day itself. Add in the costs of professional-grade equipment, and the price starts to make sense. That said, be cautious when you come across someone charging far below the industry standard, especially during peak wedding season. If a photographer or videographer is offering their services for less than $1,000, it may be a red flag. They might lack professional training or experience in the unique demands of wedding photography. Worse, issues like unreliability, unprofessional behavior, or inadequate equipment can quickly turn your special day into a stressful experience. I've heard my fair share of horror stories from couples who tried to cut costs. At one wedding I worked at, a bridesmaid told me that her photographer lost the SD card with all her wedding photos, leaving her without any memories of the day. Another couple shared how it took over six months—and multiple angry calls—to finally receive their photos. If your budget is tight, it's often better to skip hiring an inexperienced amateur altogether; although you could get lucky, many of them should be working as an assistant to someone that has worked weddings so they learn from someone that knows what they are doing, not handling the weddings themselves and learning as they go along. Instead, if you're in this scenario of wanting to save money, consider asking a friend or family member to take photos on a good smartphone or basic camera. Later in this book, I'll include tips for DIY wedding photography and advice on posing to look your best. With a little planning and effort, you can still capture meaningful, beautiful memories without the risk of hiring someone who doesn't know what they're doing.
- If you want to hire a professional photographer or videographer but have a limited budget, consider opting for shorter coverage times. Instead of paying for the entire day, focus on capturing the most

important moments, like the ceremony, family portraits, and key highlights from the start of the reception and have your cake cutting and first dances before the dinner. For example, my company offers half-day packages, in addition to full-day options. Many other professionals offer similar packages, and these can be a great way to save money while still ensuring quality coverage of your big day. If the photographer or videographer you want to hire doesn't advertise half-day rates, don't hesitate to ask if they'd be willing to customize a package for you. If they're unable or unwilling to accommodate, remember that there are likely dozens of other talented professionals who do offer half-day options and would love to be part of your wedding. The key is to find someone whose work you love and whose services align with your budget. I'll include more details in the DIY section at the end of this book on finding the vendors that are right for you.

8. Simplify the Floral Budget

- Choose in-season flowers or greenery-heavy arrangements to reduce costs.
- Repurpose ceremony decor for the reception to get double the use.

9. Cut Down on Printed Stationery

- Use digital save-the-dates and invitations to save on printing and postage costs.
- Skip extras like RSVP cards by using a wedding website or Google Forms for guest responses.

10. Borrow or Upcycle

- Borrow items like decor, jewelry, or even table linens from family or friends.
- Use heirloom pieces or repurpose items you already own for a personal, cost-effective touch.

11. Skip the Extras

- Forego expensive party favors—most guests won't miss them.
- Choose a simple yet elegant cake design and avoid multiple-tiered creations or elaborate fondant designs.

12. Book Local Vendors

- Hiring vendors who are local to your venue can cut travel costs and fees. For example, I charge up to $5,000 plus airfare and hotel costs for wedding photography in cities such as Tokyo, London, New York and San Francisco, but only $1,500 to $2,000 in the Midwest. Finding someone local can help you find a much more reasonable price. Keep in mind, many of the services that list photographers such as Wedding Wire, Google or Thumbtack charge very expensive fees to be seen on their platforms, meaning, the photographers that are on them have to charge much higher prices than someone that is not using them; and you can sometimes find much more reasonable rates by looking up someone from your state's local professional photography association, which will generally have a list and contact info of a photographer near you.
- Ask for recommendations from friends or family to find talented vendors at lower prices.

By making thoughtful choices and focusing on what matters most to you, you can create a wedding that's both cost-effective and unforgettable. Saving money doesn't mean compromising on your vision—it means being resourceful and intentional about the details that make your day special.

Choosing the Date

Selecting your wedding date is one of the first big decisions you'll make during the planning process. The date you choose will influence nearly every aspect of your wedding, from the venue and vendors to the theme and overall vibe. Here's how to approach this crucial step with confidence, keeping seasonal considerations, availability, and significance in mind.

---

1. Seasonal Considerations

Every season brings its own charm—and challenges. Here's what to keep in mind when choosing your wedding season:

- Spring: Known for blooming flowers and mild weather, spring is a popular choice. However, it's also peak wedding season, which can drive up prices and reduce vendor availability.
- Summer: Perfect for outdoor weddings, but be prepared for heat, humidity, and higher travel costs for guests. Beaches and destination weddings are common in this season.
- Fall: A favorite for its cozy, romantic vibes and stunning foliage. Autumn is also a busy wedding season, so book venues and vendors well in advance.
- Winter: A budget-friendly option, especially if you opt for a weekday or off-season date. Winter weddings can feel magical, but weather conditions may pose challenges for travel.

2. Venue and Vendor Availability

Your chosen date may hinge on the availability of your preferred venue and vendors. Keep these tips in mind:

- Start Early: Popular venues can book up a year or more in advance, especially for weekends during peak wedding seasons.
- Be Flexible: If your dream venue isn't available on your preferred date, consider a weekday or an off-peak time of year.
- Ask About Discounts: Many venues offer reduced rates for weekday, morning, or off-season weddings.

3. Significance of the Date

Make your wedding day even more meaningful by selecting a date with personal or cultural significance:

- Anniversaries or Milestones: Consider a date tied to your relationship, like the day you met, your engagement date, or another meaningful occasion.
- Family Traditions: Some couples choose dates that honor family heritage or cultural significance.
- Astrological or Symbolic Dates: Certain couples enjoy choosing dates with numerological or symbolic meaning, such as 2/22/22 or 11/11.
- Holidays and Long Weekends: A holiday wedding can be convenient for guests traveling from out of town, but it may also come with increased travel and accommodation costs.

4. Practical Considerations

- Guest Availability: Consider how your date might affect your guest list. For instance, holiday weekends or weekdays could pose challenges for some guests.
- Weather: Research the typical weather patterns for your desired time of year and location. Be prepared with a backup plan for outdoor weddings.
- Budget Impact: Certain dates, such as Saturdays during peak seasons, tend to be more expensive. Opting for a weekday or an off-peak season can save significant costs.

5. Give Yourself Enough Time

While you may be eager to tie the knot, giving yourself ample time to plan can reduce stress and ensure your dream day comes together. A general guideline:

- Short Engagement (3-6 months): Works well for small, simple weddings.
- Typical Engagement (12-18 months): Offers enough time to book vendors, secure your venue, and save for your big day.
- Long Engagement (2+ years): Ideal for elaborate weddings or when saving for the event requires more time.

Final Tip: Choose What Feels Right

Your wedding date is more than just a day—it's the starting point for your next chapter. Whether you prioritize weather, availability, or a sentimental connection, what matters most is that the date feels right for you and your partner.

P.S. If there is someone you don't like but have to invite to the wedding, but know they have to work a certain day they can't get out of: *consider that day for your wedding.*

A Cautionary (and Hilarious) Tale
On a lighter note, I once had a couple ask if I could Photoshop someone out of all their wedding photos. Their reasoning? This particular guest was "that condescending older sibling" who had a history of tormenting the groom as a kid—most notably by farting in their face, even while they were sleeping, and clearing out entire rooms of people during Thanksgiving dinners and blaming it on the turkey. They shared that the sibling's pranks had continued into adulthood, and they believed their mischievous behavior was in full force on their wedding day, allegedly "intentionally farting throughout the event and walking away like nothing happened each time."

The couple didn't want their wedding album immortalizing the siblings' mischievous grins, as they were convinced it was all part of an effort to poop on their big day. While this is definitely one of the more unusual requests I've received, it's a reminder that weddings can bring out all sorts of emotions—and sometimes a bit of family drama!

Finding the Venue

Your venue sets the tone for your wedding and is often the first major decision you'll make in the planning process. It's where your vision comes to life, so it's crucial to choose a location that aligns with your style, accommodates your guests, and fits within your budget. This section will help you navigate the key factors to consider, along with a checklist and questions to ask when touring potential venues.

Factors to Consider

1. **Location**
    - Choose a venue that's convenient for the majority of your guests.
    - Consider proximity to airports, hotels, or public transportation for out-of-town attendees.
    - Think about logistics: Is there ample parking or valet service?
2. **Size and Capacity**
    - Ensure the venue comfortably accommodates your guest list.
    - For intimate weddings, avoid oversized venues that may feel empty. Conversely, don't overcrowd a small space with a large guest count.
3. **Theme and Style**
    - Does the venue match your wedding theme (rustic, modern, romantic, etc.)?
    - Consider existing decor and ambiance—this can save money on decorations if the space already aligns with your vision.
4. **Indoor vs. Outdoor Options**
    - For outdoor venues, ensure there's a backup plan in case of bad weather (e.g., tents or an indoor alternative).
    - Check if the venue provides heating or air conditioning for seasonal comfort.
5. **Budget**
    - Confirm the rental fee and what it includes (tables, chairs, linens, etc.).
    - Understand additional costs like service fees, taxes, or overtime charges.
6. **Restrictions**
    - Check if there are noise restrictions, curfews, or rules about decor (e.g., no open flames or confetti).
    - Some venues have exclusive vendor lists, which could impact your options.
7. **Accessibility**
    - Ensure the venue is accessible for guests with mobility challenges.
    - Check for ramps, elevators, and accessible restrooms.

Venue Checklist for Tours

Use this checklist to evaluate potential venues:

- Does the venue fit your budget?
- Is the location convenient for most guests?
- Can it comfortably accommodate your guest count?
- Does it align with your wedding theme or style?

- Are both indoor and outdoor options available?
- Is there a backup plan for weather or other emergencies?
- What's included in the rental fee (tables, chairs, lighting, decor)?
- Are there restrictions on vendors, decor, or timing?
- Is the venue accessible for all guests?
- Are there parking or transportation options for guests?
- What's the cancellation or refund policy?

Questions to Ask During Venue Tours

1. **Availability and Logistics**
   - Is my preferred date available?
   - How many events do you host on the same day?
   - What's the setup and teardown schedule?
2. **Pricing and Fees**
   - What's included in the rental fee?
   - Are there additional charges (e.g., security, cleaning, overtime)?
   - What's the deposit amount, and when is the balance due?
3. **Vendor Policies**
   - Do you have a preferred vendor list?
   - Can I bring in outside vendors, including caterers and bartenders?
   - Are there kitchen facilities for catering staff?
4. **Amenities and Services**
   - Do you provide tables, chairs, linens, or decor?
   - Are sound systems or microphones included?
   - Is there a bridal suite or preparation area for the wedding party?
5. **Guest Experience**
   - What's the parking situation? Is valet or shuttle service available?
   - Are there accommodations nearby for out-of-town guests?
   - Are restrooms clean, accessible, and sufficient for my guest count?
6. **Weather and Emergencies**
   - For outdoor weddings, what's the rain plan?
   - Do you provide staff to assist with any unexpected issues during the event?

Final Tip: Trust Your Gut

After touring a venue, think about how it made you feel. Did it spark excitement? Could you envision your big day there? Practical considerations are essential, but your gut instinct often knows best.

Building Your Guest List

Your guest list is the foundation of your wedding planning—it influences everything from the venue size to your catering costs. Deciding who to invite can be one of the most challenging parts of the process, but with a clear strategy, you can build a guest list that reflects your vision for the day. Here's how to approach it step by step, plus tips for managing RSVPs and navigating the occasional politics that come with wedding invitations.

Step 1: Define Your Vision

Before diving into names, determine the overall vibe of your wedding. Is it an intimate gathering or a grand celebration? This will help you set parameters for your guest list:

- Intimate Weddings (up to 50 guests): Focus on immediate family and close friends.
- Medium-Sized Weddings (50-150 guests): Include extended family, coworkers, and additional friends.
- Large Weddings (150+ guests): Open the list to distant relatives, acquaintances, and plus-ones.

Step 2: Start with Your Inner Circle

Write down the people who are essential to your day:

- Immediate family (parents, siblings, grandparents).
- Closest friends who feel like family.
- Anyone who has played a significant role in your relationship.

Once you have these names, work outward to include extended family, friends, and coworkers as space and budget allow.

Step 3: Set Boundaries and Guidelines

To avoid an ever-expanding guest list, establish some clear rules:

- No Obligation Invites: Just because someone invited you to their wedding doesn't mean you have to reciprocate.
- Plus-Ones: Decide if you'll allow plus-ones for all guests or limit them to married or long-term couples.

- Children: Will your wedding be adults-only, or will you include kids? Communicate this clearly to avoid confusion.
- Coworkers: Only invite those you have a close relationship with—don't feel obligated to invite your entire office.

Step 4: Managing RSVPs

Keeping track of RSVPs can be a logistical challenge, but these tips will help:

- Set a Deadline: Include a clear RSVP date on your invitations, typically 3-4 weeks before the wedding.
- Use Digital Tools: Wedding websites or apps can make it easier to track RSVPs and meal preferences.
- Follow Up: If you haven't heard from a guest by the deadline, reach out politely to confirm their attendance.

Step 5: Navigating Tricky Guest List Politics

Weddings often come with emotional or political challenges when it comes to who gets invited. Here's how to handle common scenarios:

1. Parental Requests:
   - If parents are contributing financially, they may expect to invite their friends or extended family. Set clear limits based on your budget and capacity.
   - Offer them a set number of "slots" to use as they see fit.
2. Divorced Families:
   - Be mindful of family dynamics when inviting divorced parents or relatives who don't get along.
   - Create a seating plan that minimizes tension.
3. Uninvited Expectations:
   - If someone assumes they're invited but aren't, be honest but kind: "We'd love to have everyone, but due to space and budget, we've had to make tough decisions about the guest list."
4. Last-Minute Requests:
   - Politely decline late additions, explaining that plans are already finalized.

Step 6: Keep a Buffer List

Create a secondary list of "maybe" guests. If people from your initial list decline, you can extend invitations to those on the buffer list without overextending your budget.

Step 7: Stay True to Your Vision

Remember, your wedding day is about celebrating your love and commitment. Don't let external pressures derail your vision. Invite the people who matter most to you and your partner, and trust that your celebration will be meaningful, regardless of the size of the guest list.

Part 2: Creating the Look and Feel

Now that you've laid the groundwork for your wedding—budget, date, venue, and guest list—it's time to dive into the creative side of planning: crafting the look and feel of your big day. This is where your vision comes to life, blending your personal style with thoughtful details that make the event truly yours. From designing invitations to selecting decor and attire, this section will guide you step-by-step through the elements that set the mood and create a lasting impression for you and your guests.

What to Expect in This Section

1. **Crafting Invitations and Save-the-Dates**
   - Designing and wording your invitations.
   - Timing tips for sending save-the-dates and invitations.
2. **Dreaming Up Your Decor**
   - Exploring themes, colors, and personal touches.
   - Working with florists, rental companies, or DIYing your decor.
3. **Finding the Perfect Dress (and Attire for Everyone Else)**
   - Shopping tips for bridal wear, wedding party attire, and guest dress codes.
   - Managing fittings, alterations, and comfort on the big day.
4. **Floral and Decor Arrangements**
   - Choosing flowers that suit your theme, season, and budget.
   - Ideas for repurposing ceremony decor for the reception.

This part of the book will help you focus on the creative details that transform your wedding from an event into an experience. Whether your style is timeless elegance, rustic charm, or something uniquely yours, you'll find practical advice and inspiration to bring your vision to life.

Let's get started by crafting your invitations and save-the-dates!

Crafting Invitations and Save-the-Dates

Your invitations and save-the-dates are the first glimpse your guests will have of your wedding day. They set the tone for your celebration and provide important details about your event. Whether you're going for classic elegance, whimsical charm, or something totally unique, this section will guide you through selecting the perfect designs, choosing the right wording, and staying on top of timing and RSVPs.

Selecting Designs, Paper Types, and Wording

1. **Choosing a Design**
   - Reflect Your Theme: Match your invitations and save-the-dates to your wedding's theme and color palette. For example, elegant script and metallic accents work well for formal weddings, while floral or minimalist designs complement rustic or casual events.
   - Consider Customization: Many online platforms offer customizable templates, or you can work with a designer for something one-of-a-kind.
2. **Picking the Right Materials**
   - Paper Types: Opt for high-quality cardstock, vellum, or recycled paper for a polished look. If you want something extra special, consider textured paper, letterpress printing, or foil stamping.
   - Eco-Friendly Options: Digital invitations or plantable seed paper can be great choices if sustainability is important to you.
3. **Wording Your Invitations**
   - Save-the-Dates: Keep them simple and straightforward—include your names, the wedding date, and a note that a formal invitation will follow.
   - Invitations: Include essential details like the date, time, venue, and RSVP instructions. Be sure to match the tone of your wedding. For example:
     - *Formal:* "The honor of your presence is requested..."
     - *Casual:* "Join us for a celebration of love!"

Timing for Sending Invitations and Tracking RSVPs

1. **When to Send Save-the-Dates**
   - Destination Weddings: 8-12 months before the event to give guests ample time to plan travel and accommodations.
   - Local Weddings: 6-8 months in advance is usually sufficient.
2. **When to Send Invitations**
   - Destination Weddings: 4-6 months before the wedding.
   - Local Weddings: 6-8 weeks before the event.
3. **Tracking RSVPs**
   - Set a Clear Deadline: Request RSVPs 3-4 weeks before your wedding date to give you enough time to finalize guest counts with your vendors.
   - Include RSVP Instructions: Provide clear instructions on how to RSVP, whether it's via mail, email, or a wedding website.
   - Use Technology: Wedding websites or apps can make RSVP tracking much easier. You can also ask for meal preferences and note any dietary restrictions.

- Follow Up Politely: If you haven't received a response by the deadline, reach out with a gentle reminder.

Final Tip: Make It Personal

Your invitations are an opportunity to share a piece of your story as a couple. Whether it's incorporating a meaningful quote, a monogram, or artwork inspired by your relationship, small personal touches can make your stationery feel even more special.

Dreaming Up Your Decor

Your decor is a powerful way to set the mood and reflect your personal style on your wedding day. Whether you're envisioning a timeless, elegant affair or a playful, whimsical celebration, this is where you can let your creativity shine. This section will guide you through finding inspiration for themes, selecting colors, adding personal touches, and collaborating with florists and rental companies to bring your vision to life.

Inspiration for Themes, Colors, and Personalized Touches

1. **Choosing a Theme**
    - **Classic Elegance:** Think neutral colors, luxurious fabrics, and understated centerpieces.
    - **Rustic Charm:** Incorporate wood accents, mason jars, and earthy tones.
    - **Romantic and Vintage:** Opt for pastel shades, lace details, and antique-inspired decor.
    - **Modern Minimalism:** Use clean lines, monochromatic palettes, and sleek furniture.
    - **Destination Inspired:** Infuse elements of your chosen location, such as tropical florals for a beach wedding or rustic lanterns for a mountain celebration.
2. **Selecting a Color Palette**
    - Start with one or two base colors and add complementary accents. For example:
        - Navy blue and gold for a formal look.
        - Blush and greenery for a romantic vibe.
        - Terracotta and rust for a trendy, bohemian feel.
    - Consider seasonal colors—soft pastels for spring, bold jewel tones for autumn, or icy blues for winter.
3. **Adding Personalized Touches**
    - Incorporate your love story into the decor:
        - Use photos from your relationship as table numbers.
        - Name tables after places you've traveled together.
    - Include cultural or family traditions in your decor.

- Create a signature piece, like a custom neon sign, that can double as a keepsake.

Working with Florists and Rental Companies

1. **Collaborating with Florists**
    - **Bring Your Vision to Life:** Share your color palette, theme, and inspiration photos with your florist.
    - **Be Open to Suggestions:** Trust your florist's expertise, especially when it comes to seasonal flowers or budget-friendly alternatives.
    - **Repurpose Arrangements:** Maximize your budget by using ceremony florals for reception decor. For example, aisle arrangements can double as table centerpieces.
    - **Discuss the Details:** Confirm delivery times, setup, and tear-down responsibilities to avoid last-minute surprises.
2. **Working with Rental Companies**
    - **What to Rent:** Consider renting items like furniture, tableware, linens, lighting, and specialty decor pieces to elevate your venue's look.
    - **Mix and Match:** Combine rented items with DIY or purchased decor for a more personalized feel.
    - **Compare Options:** Visit rental showrooms if possible to see and touch the items before making decisions.
    - **Ask About Packages:** Many companies offer bundled pricing for multiple items, which can save you money.
    - **Coordinate Pickup and Return:** Confirm who is responsible for transport and ensure it aligns with your timeline.

Final Tip: Stay True to Your Vision

Remember, your decor doesn't have to be over-the-top to make an impact. What matters most is that it reflects you as a couple and creates an atmosphere where you and your guests can celebrate comfortably and joyfully. Whether it's lush floral arrangements, handmade accents, or subtle details that hold personal meaning, every element should feel like a piece of your story.

Finding the Perfect Dress (and Attire for Everyone Else)

Choosing what to wear on your wedding day is one of the most exciting—and sometimes stressful—parts of the planning process. Your attire should reflect your personal style, suit the tone of your wedding, and, most importantly, make you feel confident and comfortable. This section will guide you through bridal dress shopping, alterations, and attire options for the wedding party, along with tips for setting a dress code for your guests.

A Guide to Bridal Dress Shopping and Alterations

1. **Start Early**
    - Begin dress shopping 9-12 months before your wedding day. Custom or made-to-order gowns can take several months to arrive, and you'll need time for alterations.
    - If you're short on time, consider off-the-rack options or sample sales.
2. **Do Your Research**
    - Browse bridal magazines, Pinterest, and Instagram for inspiration. Save photos of styles, fabrics, and silhouettes you love.
    - Learn the terminology: Know the difference between A-line, ballgown, mermaid, and sheath styles to communicate your preferences effectively. Descriptions of each are below at the end of this sub-section.
3. **Set a Budget**
    - Factor in the cost of the dress, alterations, accessories (veil, shoes, jewelry), and any preservation services for after the wedding.
    - Be upfront about your budget with the bridal salon to avoid trying on dresses out of your price range.
4. **The Shopping Experience**
    - Book appointments at bridal salons and bring trusted friends or family members whose opinions you value.
    - Wear undergarments and bring shoes with a similar heel height to what you plan to wear on your wedding day.
5. **Alterations**
    - Expect to schedule 2-3 fittings. The first fitting ensures the dress fits your body, while subsequent fittings perfect the details.
    - Be sure to move around, sit, and dance during fittings to test the comfort and fit of the dress.
    - Bring all accessories, including your veil and shoes, to fittings to get the full look.

A-Line

- **Description:** The A-line dress is fitted at the bodice and gradually flares out from the waist, resembling the shape of an "A."
- **Why It Works:** This universally flattering style suits most body types and is a timeless, versatile choice.
- **Best For:** Brides who want a classic, elegant look without excessive volume.

Ballgown

- **Description:** Often called the "princess dress," the ballgown features a fitted bodice and a dramatic, full skirt.
- **Why It Works:** The voluminous skirt adds drama and grandeur, while the fitted bodice emphasizes the waist.
- **Best For:** Formal or fairy-tale weddings and brides who want to create a glamorous, regal impression.

Mermaid

- **Description:** The mermaid dress hugs the body from the chest to the knees, then flares out dramatically at or below the knees.
- **Why It Works:** It highlights curves and creates a sultry, hourglass silhouette.
- **Best For:** Brides who want to showcase their figure and embrace a sexy, dramatic style.

Sheath

- **Description:** The sheath dress features a slim, straight silhouette that flows naturally from the neckline to the hem, without flaring out.
- **Why It Works:** Its minimalist design creates a modern, sleek look and is perfect for showcasing lightweight fabrics.
- **Best For:** Beach or destination weddings, petite brides, or those seeking a simple, understated elegance.

Additional Wedding Dress Silhouettes

1. **Trumpet**
   - **Description:** Similar to the mermaid style, but the flare begins higher, around mid-thigh, creating a softer transition.
   - **Why It Works:** Offers a balance between highlighting curves and allowing more freedom of movement.

- **Best For:** Brides who want a glamorous look with a touch of elegance without the dramatic flair of a mermaid gown.
2. **Empire**
    - **Description:** The empire dress features a high waistline just below the bust, with the skirt flowing straight down.
    - **Why It Works:** It creates a long, flowing silhouette and draws attention upward, elongating the body.
    - **Best For:** Petite brides, brides with a smaller bust, or those seeking a comfortable, flowing design.
3. **Tea-Length**
    - **Description:** A vintage-inspired style where the hem falls between the knee and ankle, offering a playful yet classic look.
    - **Why It Works:** Perfect for showcasing shoes and adding a retro vibe.
    - **Best For:** Casual, outdoor, or brunch weddings, as well as brides who want a unique, flirty look.
4. **Fit-and-Flare**
    - **Description:** A toned-down version of the trumpet, this style fits snugly through the bodice and hips before subtly flaring out.
    - **Why It Works:** Offers a flattering shape without the dramatic flair of a mermaid or trumpet gown.
    - **Best For:** Brides who want a slightly curvy silhouette without feeling restricted.
5. **Short Dresses**
    - **Description:** Dresses with hemlines above the knee or just below.
    - **Why It Works:** A modern, unconventional choice perfect for a casual or summer wedding.
    - **Best For:** Informal ceremonies, second weddings, or brides who want something lightweight and easy to move in.

Choosing the Right Silhouette Based on Body Type

1. **Hourglass (Balanced Bust and Hips with a Defined Waist)**
    - **Best Silhouettes:** Mermaid, trumpet, fit-and-flare, and ballgown.
    - **Why:** These styles highlight your curves and draw attention to your naturally defined waistline.
2. **Pear Shape (Wider Hips, Narrower Bust and Shoulders)**
    - **Best Silhouettes:** A-line, ballgown, and empire.
    - **Why:** These styles balance proportions by accentuating the upper body and softly skimming over the hips.

3. **Apple Shape (Wider Midsection with Slimmer Legs)**
   - **Best Silhouettes:** Empire, A-line, and ballgown.
   - **Why:** These styles draw attention upward and create a flattering, elongated silhouette.
4. **Petite (Shorter Stature with Smaller Frame)**
   - **Best Silhouettes:** Sheath, empire, and trumpet.
   - **Why:** These styles avoid overwhelming a smaller frame and create the illusion of height.
5. **Tall (Longer Torso and/or Legs)**
   - **Best Silhouettes:** A-line, sheath, and ballgown.
   - **Why:** These styles complement a tall figure without adding unnecessary length.
6. **Plus Size (Curvier Frame, Proportional or Pear-Shaped)**
   - **Best Silhouettes:** A-line, ballgown, and empire.
   - **Why:** These styles provide support, emphasize the waist, and enhance curves beautifully.
7. **Athletic (Straight Figure, Subtle Curves)**
   - **Best Silhouettes:** Mermaid, trumpet, and sheath.
   - **Why:** These styles add curves and highlight a toned physique.

Pro Tips for Finding Your Perfect Dress

- **Comfort First:** Choose a dress you can move, sit, and dance in comfortably.
- **Emphasize What You Love:** Highlight your favorite features, whether it's your shoulders, back, or waist.
- **Take Photos at Fittings:** Seeing yourself in photos can help you decide what feels most flattering.
- **Trust the Fitters:** A skilled bridal consultant can help you find styles you may not have considered that suit your body shape.
- **Tailoring Matters:** The perfect dress is all about the fit. Don't shy away from alterations to customize the gown to your body.

The Shopping Experience: Top Retailers and Budget-Friendly Options

Finding your dream wedding dress doesn't have to break the bank. Whether you're shopping at high-end bridal salons, online retailers, or exploring resale and rental options, there's a perfect gown for every budget. This section highlights the best places to start your search, from top retailers to affordable alternatives.

Top Bridal Retailers

If you're looking for a traditional bridal shopping experience with a range of styles and budgets, these well-known retailers are great places to start:

1. **David's Bridal**
    - **Why It's Popular:** Offers a wide range of styles, sizes (including plus-size), and prices, with dresses starting as low as $99.
    - **Extras:** Bridesmaid dresses, accessories, and in-house alterations.
    - **Where to Shop:** Nationwide locations and online at davidsbridal.com.
2. **BHLDN (Anthropologie's Bridal Line)**
    - **Why It's Popular:** Known for bohemian, romantic designs that are stylish and modern.
    - **Price Range:** $800–$3,000.
    - **Where to Shop:** Select Anthropologie stores and online at bhldn.com.
3. **Kleinfeld Bridal**
    - **Why It's Popular:** Famous from *Say Yes to the Dress*, Kleinfeld offers a luxurious shopping experience and exclusive designer collections.
    - **Price Range:** $2,000–$10,000+.
    - **Where to Shop:** New York City showroom or online at kleinfeldbridal.com.
4. **Maggie Sottero**
    - **Why It's Popular:** A leading designer offering elegant, customizable dresses with intricate details.
    - **Price Range:** $800–$3,500.
    - **Where to Shop:** Available at authorized bridal salons worldwide. Use their store locator at maggiesottero.com.
5. **Pronovias**
    - **Why It's Popular:** Known for high-end, European-style wedding gowns that are timeless and chic.
    - **Price Range:** $1,500–$5,000.
    - **Where to Shop:** Bridal salons and Pronovias boutiques, or online at pronovias.com.

Online Retailers for Convenience and Budget Shopping

1. **Azazie**
    - **Why It's Great:** Affordable, customizable dresses with a try-before-you-buy option.
    - **Price Range:** $199–$800.
    - **Where to Shop:** azazie.com.
2. **Lulus Bridal**
    - **Why It's Great:** Budget-friendly options for modern, minimalist brides.
    - **Price Range:** $50–$300.

- **Where to Shop:** lulus.com.
3. **Etsy**
    - **Why It's Great:** Unique, handmade dresses from independent designers, often at lower prices.
    - **Price Range:** $200–$2,000.
    - **Where to Shop:** etsy.com.
4. **ASOS Bridal**
    - **Why It's Great:** Affordable, trendy styles for fashion-forward brides.
    - **Price Range:** $100–$500.
    - **Where to Shop:** asos.com.
5. **Stillwhite**
    - **Why It's Great:** A marketplace for pre-owned wedding dresses, including designer options at a fraction of the original cost.
    - **Price Range:** $300–$2,500.
    - **Where to Shop:** stillwhite.com.

Resale, Rental, and Budget-Friendly Options

1. **Pre-Owned Wedding Dresses**
    - **Stillwhite, Nearly Newlywed, OnceWed:** These platforms offer gently used or sample gowns at significantly reduced prices. Perfect for finding a designer dress on a budget.
2. **Rentals**
    - **Rent the Runway:** Offers elegant bridal and bridesmaid dresses for rent.
    - **Lending Luxury:** Specializes in renting gowns for special occasions, including weddings.
3. **Consignment Shops and Sample Sales**
    - **Consignment Stores:** Local consignment shops often have wedding dresses in excellent condition at bargain prices.
    - **Sample Sales:** Many bridal salons hold sample sales, where floor models and discontinued styles are sold at steep discounts.
4. **Thrift Stores**
    - **Goodwill and Local Thrift Shops:** With patience, you may uncover a vintage or gently used dress for a fraction of retail prices.

How to Find Local Niche Bridal Boutiques in Your City

Finding a niche bridal boutique in your city can provide a more personal, tailored experience compared to larger chain stores. These boutiques often carry unique or hard-to-find styles, making them a great option for brides who want something special. Here are tips for discovering the perfect boutique near you:

1. Start with a Local Search

- Use search terms like *"bridal boutique near me," "independent bridal shop [city],"* or *"wedding dress boutique [city]."*
- Check Google Maps for highly rated shops and read recent reviews to get a sense of their style and service quality.

2. Explore Social Media

- Search hashtags like *#BridalBoutique[City]* or *#WeddingDress[City]* on Instagram to find shops showcasing their collections.
- Follow local bridal shops and designers—they often post photos of their latest gowns, trunk shows, or special events.

3. Ask for Recommendations

- Reach out to local wedding planners or photographers—they often have firsthand experience with boutiques and can recommend trusted shops.
- Join wedding planning groups on Facebook or Reddit (e.g., r/WeddingPlanning) and ask for recommendations specific to your city.

4. Check Bridal Shows and Expos

- Attend local bridal shows or expos, where boutique owners often showcase their gowns and provide information about their shop.

5. Look for Specialized Services

- Some boutiques cater to specific styles or needs, such as vintage-inspired gowns, boho designs, or inclusive sizing. Look for shops that advertise these specialties if you have a specific vision in mind.
- If you're searching for eco-friendly or sustainable dresses, look for keywords like *"ethical bridal shop [city]"* or *"sustainable wedding dresses [city]."*

6. Visit Local Shopping Districts

- Many cities have neighborhoods or streets known for boutique shopping. Walk through these areas, as smaller bridal shops are often tucked away in charming locations.

7. Expand to Nearby Cities or Suburbs

- If you're not finding the right boutique in your city, explore options in nearby cities or suburbs. Smaller towns often have hidden gems with a more relaxed shopping atmosphere and lower prices.

8. Browse Bridal Directories

- Use specialized bridal directories like:
    - **The Knot** (theknot.com)
    - **WeddingWire** (weddingwire.com)
    - **Bridal Boutiques US** (bridalboutiques.us)

    These platforms allow you to filter by location and read reviews from past brides.

Tips for Shopping on a Very Low Budget

- **Start Early:** The more time you have, the better your chances of finding a great deal.
- **Keep Alterations in Mind:** A bargain dress may need alterations, so budget for these costs.
- **Simplify Your Vision:** Look for classic, simple styles that are easier to tailor and accessorize.
- **DIY Personalization:** Add your own flair with belts, appliques, or custom veils.

Options for the Wedding Party and Guest Dress Codes

1. **Dressing the Wedding Party**
    - **Bridesmaids:** Decide whether you want matching dresses, a mix-and-match palette, or individual styles within a cohesive color scheme. Be mindful of your bridesmaids' budgets and body types.
    - **Groomsmen:** Coordinate their attire with the overall theme. Options range from classic tuxedos to more relaxed suits or even suspenders and bow ties for a rustic vibe.

- **Parents of the Couple:** Offer guidance but allow them to choose attire that makes them feel comfortable and confident. Ensure their outfits align with the formality and colors of the wedding.
2. **Setting a Dress Code for Guests**
    - **Formal/Black Tie:** Tuxedos and floor-length gowns.
    - **Semi-Formal:** Suits, cocktail dresses, or dressy separates.
    - **Casual:** Sundresses, khakis, button-ups—perfect for outdoor or beach weddings.
    - **Themed Dress Code:** Add a fun twist by incorporating your wedding's theme into the attire (e.g., vintage, garden party, or festive colors).
3. **Communicating the Dress Code**
    - Include the dress code on your invitations, wedding website, or both. Be clear and specific to avoid confusion. For example:
        - "Black Tie: Formal evening wear is requested."
        - "Beach Chic: Sundresses and linen shirts encouraged—sandals welcome!"
    - If you're concerned about guests dressing inappropriately, add helpful style tips on your wedding website to give them guidance.

Final Tip: Keep Comfort in Mind

Whether it's your wedding gown, your bridesmaids' dresses, or the groomsmen's attire, comfort is key. You'll be wearing these outfits for hours, so ensure they allow you to move, dance, and enjoy the day without restrictions. And remember, the most important thing is that you feel like the best version of yourself when you say, "I do."

Outfit Tips for Wedding and Bridesmaids' Dresses

1. For Wedding Dresses:

- **Choose the Right Silhouette:**
    - **A-Line Dresses:** Universally flattering, as they cinch at the waist and flow outward, creating balance and elegance.
    - **Empire Waist:** Ideal for elongating the frame and minimizing attention on the midsection.
    - **Fit-and-Flare or Mermaid:** Best for highlighting curves while still offering structure.
    - **Ballgown:** Great for creating a dramatic, princess-like effect while emphasizing the waist.
- **Fabric Matters:**
    - Heavier fabrics like satin or mikado provide structure and smoothness.
    - Flowing fabrics like chiffon or tulle add softness and romance.

- Avoid overly clingy fabrics if you're concerned about highlighting certain areas.
- **Focus on the Waist:**
    - A well-defined waist creates a flattering silhouette. Consider dresses with belts, sashes, or cinched waists for added definition.
- **Sleeve Options:**
    - Cap sleeves or illusion sleeves provide a delicate, elegant touch for those who want more arm coverage.
    - Long lace sleeves add timeless sophistication.
    - Off-the-shoulder styles emphasize the collarbone and shoulders.
- **Train Length:**
    - A long train adds drama but may feel overwhelming for petite brides. Opt for a shorter train or a detachable one if you want more freedom of movement.
- **Neckline Details:**
    - Sweetheart necklines soften the bust line and add a romantic touch.
    - Illusion necklines provide coverage without looking bulky.
    - Halter necklines work well for highlighting toned shoulders and arms.

2. For Bridesmaids' Dresses:

- **Let Them Choose Their Style:**
    - Offer options within the same color palette or fabric to suit different body types. For example, allow variations like strapless, halter, or cap-sleeve designs.
    - Convertible dresses are a great choice, as they can be styled differently for each bridesmaid.
- **Flattering Features for All Shapes:**
    - Empire waists flatter a variety of figures.
    - Midi or tea-length dresses are great for both formal and casual weddings.
    - Wrap dresses offer flexibility and fit most body types beautifully.
- **Keep Comfort in Mind:**
    - Opt for fabrics that breathe, like chiffon or jersey, especially for outdoor weddings.
    - Avoid fabrics that easily wrinkle or show sweat, such as certain satins or silks, for hot-weather weddings.
- **Accessories as Enhancers:**
    - Use statement jewelry, belts, or hairpieces to tie the look together while allowing individuality.

3. Universal Tips for Bridal Party Attire:

- **Color Considerations:**
    - Choose shades that complement a variety of skin tones (e.g., jewel tones like emerald, navy, and burgundy tend to flatter everyone).
    - Avoid overly bright or neon colors that may not photograph well.

- **Match the Wedding Aesthetic:**
  - For a rustic wedding, consider lighter fabrics and muted tones.
  - For formal black-tie weddings, full-length gowns in rich colors or metallics add elegance.
- **Comfortable Footwear:**
  - Choose shoes that are comfortable enough for a long day. Bridesmaids can switch to flats or sandals during the reception if needed.
  - Ensure the height of the shoes works with the length of the dresses—no one wants a tripping hazard!

Coordinating Styles for the Wedding Party

1. **Consistency with Flexibility**
   - **Match the Palette, Not the Style:** Allow bridesmaids to choose dresses in the same color family but in different styles (e.g., one-shoulder, strapless, or sleeved) to suit their body types and preferences.
   - **Fabric Consistency:** Keep everyone in the same fabric (e.g., chiffon or satin) to ensure the overall look is cohesive even with varied dress styles.
   - **Tie the Party Together:** Coordinate the groomsmen's attire with the bridesmaids by matching ties, pocket squares, or boutonnieres to the bridesmaids' dresses.
2. **Balance Formality**
   - Make sure the formality of the attire aligns with the venue and theme. For example:
     - A ballgown for the bride pairs well with full-length gowns for bridesmaids in formal weddings.
     - Casual weddings may feature shorter bridesmaid dresses or more relaxed fabrics, like cotton or jersey.
3. **Unity with Accessories**
   - Use coordinated accessories to tie everything together. For example:
     - Matching jewelry sets or hairpieces for bridesmaids.
     - Boutonnieres or ties in the same palette for groomsmen.
   - Add a statement accessory for the bride to stand out, such as a veil with lace detailing or a jeweled belt.
4. **Blend with the Venue Aesthetic**
   - A beach wedding calls for light, flowing dresses and linen suits.
   - A rustic barn setting may suit bohemian or earth-toned attire.
   - A grand ballroom works best with classic, formal outfits like tuxedos and gowns.

Choosing Colors for Different Seasons

1. **Spring Weddings**
   - **Colors:** Soft pastels like blush pink, lavender, baby blue, mint green, and peach.
   - **Why It Works:** These colors mirror the fresh, delicate feel of spring blooms and new beginnings.
   - **Tips:** Pair pastel dresses with light-colored or floral accessories, and consider adding subtle metallic accents like gold or rose gold.
2. **Summer Weddings**
   - **Colors:** Bright and bold shades such as coral, fuchsia, turquoise, sunny yellow, or vibrant greens.
   - **Why It Works:** These colors pop beautifully in outdoor or beach settings and reflect the cheerful vibe of summer.
   - **Tips:** Use lightweight fabrics like chiffon or linen to keep everyone cool, and opt for sandals or wedges for outdoor weddings.
3. **Fall Weddings**
   - **Colors:** Rich jewel tones like emerald green, burgundy, navy blue, mustard yellow, and burnt orange.
   - **Why It Works:** These shades complement the earthy tones of fall foliage and create a warm, cozy aesthetic.
   - **Tips:** Incorporate warm fabrics like velvet or heavier satin, and consider textured elements like lace or embroidery to enhance the seasonal feel.
4. **Winter Weddings**
   - **Colors:** Cool, icy tones like silver, navy, deep red, emerald, or even all-white ensembles.
   - **Why It Works:** These colors evoke the elegance and crispness of winter, adding a touch of sophistication to indoor venues.
   - **Tips:** Opt for long-sleeve dresses or heavier fabrics like satin or brocade to keep warm. Add faux fur stoles or capes for bridesmaids for both comfort and style.

Practical Tips for Coordinating Colors and Styles

- **Use Color Swatches:** Bring fabric swatches to planning sessions to ensure your wedding attire matches your overall decor and theme.
- **Seasonal Flowers:** Coordinate dress colors with seasonal flowers to create a seamless look in photos. For example, pastel dresses pair beautifully with spring blooms like peonies, while deep jewel tones complement fall foliage.
- **Neutral Base Colors:** If you're worried about your color scheme clashing, start with a neutral base like ivory, champagne, or gray, and add pops of color through accessories, florals, or accents.

Special Considerations for Destination Weddings

1. **Climate Matters:**
    - For tropical weddings, opt for breathable fabrics like chiffon or linen to keep everyone cool.
    - For colder destinations, consider wraps, shawls, or long-sleeve designs for warmth.
2. **Travel-Friendly Outfits:**
    - Choose wrinkle-resistant fabrics for outfits that will travel well.
    - Provide garment bags for dresses and suits to prevent damage in transit.
3. **Bold Choices for Destination Themes:**
    - Incorporate local elements into the attire, such as vibrant colors inspired by the location or accessories like floral crowns, shawls, or jewelry.

Floral and Decor Arrangements

Flowers and decor play a pivotal role in bringing your wedding's theme to life, creating an atmosphere that feels uniquely yours. Whether you're dreaming of lush bouquets, simple greenery, or bold, dramatic arrangements, this section will guide you through selecting flowers that suit your theme, season, and budget, as well as deciding between DIY options and working with a professional florist.

Selecting Flowers That Fit Your Theme, Season, and Budget

1. **Choosing Flowers for Your Theme**
    - Match your flowers to the overall vibe of your wedding:
        - **Classic Elegance:** Roses, peonies, hydrangeas, or calla lilies.
        - **Rustic Charm:** Wildflowers, sunflowers, baby's breath, or lavender.
        - **Modern Minimalism:** Orchids, succulents, or greenery-focused arrangements.
        - **Bohemian:** Pampas grass, proteas, and cascading greenery.
    - Consider the colors of your theme and choose blooms that complement your palette.
2. **Seasonal Availability**
    - Opt for in-season flowers to save on costs and ensure freshness. For example:
        - **Spring:** Tulips, daffodils, lilacs, and ranunculus.
        - **Summer:** Dahlias, zinnias, sunflowers, and roses.
        - **Fall:** Chrysanthemums, marigolds, and autumnal foliage.
        - **Winter:** Amaryllis, holly, and evergreens.
    - If your favorite flowers are out of season, ask your florist for similar alternatives.
3. **Staying Within Budget**
    - Focus on impact areas like the ceremony backdrop or centerpieces rather than covering every corner in florals.

- Incorporate greenery, which is often more affordable than flowers but just as beautiful.
- Mix real and faux flowers to save on costs while maintaining the overall look. Faux flowers can be particularly effective for large installations like arches or hanging arrangements.

Tips on DIY vs. Working with a Florist

1. **When to Go DIY**
    - DIY is ideal for smaller weddings, simple arrangements, or if you enjoy crafting.
    - Focus on easy projects, such as:
        - Mason jar centerpieces.
        - Greenery garlands for tables.
        - Single-stem bouquets or minimalist floral accents.
    - Ensure you have a team of helpers and schedule enough time before the wedding to assemble your arrangements.

DIY Checklist:

- Source flowers from wholesale markets, local farms, or online retailers.
- Invest in tools like floral tape, scissors, and foam.
- Watch tutorials or take a workshop to refine your skills.
- Practice assembling a few pieces before the wedding to avoid last-minute stress.

2. **When to Work with a Florist**
    - A florist is essential for large-scale weddings, intricate arrangements, or if you simply want to take the stress off your plate.
    - Benefits of working with a professional:
        - Access to a wider variety of flowers, including rare or exotic blooms.
        - Expert advice on seasonal options and budget-friendly alternatives.
        - Execution of complex designs, such as floral arches, hanging installations, or cascading bouquets.
    - When choosing a florist:
        - Look at their portfolio to ensure their style matches your vision.
        - Schedule a consultation to discuss your theme, budget, and priorities.
        - Confirm details such as delivery, setup, and tear-down to avoid surprises.

Final Tip: Make It Personal

Incorporate meaningful touches into your floral and decor arrangements. For example, use your grandmother's favorite flowers in your bouquet, or include blooms that symbolize qualities like love, hope, and happiness. Whether you go DIY, hire a florist, or blend both approaches, the most important thing is that your decor reflects your love story and creates an unforgettable experience for you and your guests.

Part 3: Assembling Your Dream Team

Your vendors are the backbone of your wedding day, ensuring everything runs smoothly and beautifully. From photographers and caterers to florists and DJs, the professionals you hire will play a major role in creating the wedding you've envisioned. This section will guide you through selecting, hiring, and working with vendors, so you can build a team that brings your dream day to life.

What to Expect in This Section

1. **Photography and Videography**
   - Tips for finding and hiring professionals to capture your special day.
   - Must-have shots and key moments to discuss with your team.
2. **Hiring Vendors**
   - How to choose caterers, planners, DJs, bands, and officiants.
   - Contracts, questions to ask, and managing expectations.
3. **Collaborating Effectively**
   - Tips for clear communication with vendors.
   - How to create a seamless timeline for the day of the wedding.

Your "dream team" will not only handle the details but also alleviate stress, allowing you to enjoy every moment. Let's start with one of the most important elements—capturing the memories.

Photography and Videography

Your wedding photos and videos are lasting memories that you'll treasure for years to come. Choosing the right photographer and videographer ensures these moments are captured beautifully and authentically. This section covers what to look for in professionals, as well as key shots and video moments to plan in advance.

What to Look for in a Photographer/Videographer

1. **Style and Aesthetic**
   - Look at their portfolio to determine if their style aligns with your vision:
     - **Classic/Traditional:** Timeless poses and formal group shots.
     - **Photojournalistic:** Candid, documentary-style captures of genuine moments.
     - **Artistic:** Creative angles, dramatic lighting, and unique compositions.

- **Cinematic (for videographers):** Story-driven edits with music and seamless transitions.

Many photographers, due to the constraints of reality, approach weddings with a photojournalistic style, capturing candid moments as they unfold, combined with a mix of traditional and artistic shots when time allows. Every wedding is unique, and the primary focus for most is on documenting the day as naturally as possible. Unless specifically requested, photographers typically focus on the flow of events, ensuring the basics are covered. When there's time, many photographers will stage portraits and poses for more polished, intentional photos, generally between the ceremony and reception.

It's important to keep in mind that many of the stunning images you see in wedding photographers' portfolios are often from staged shoots with professional models. These sessions allow photographers unlimited time to perfect the lighting, angles, and composition. In real-world wedding photography, however, time is often limited, and venues frequently present challenges like poor lighting or restrictions that prevent setting up ideal flash setups.

That said, the beauty of wedding photography lies in its spontaneity. Even with imperfect conditions and limited time, most weddings provide countless opportunities to capture those "perfect" moments—genuine, candid shots full of emotion and energy. These unplanned moments are often the ones that resonate most and truly tell the story of your special day. You can view real-world photos at vidart.pixieset.com for some samples.

2. **Experience and Expertise**

Hire someone experienced in weddings specifically—they'll know how to handle timelines, tricky lighting, and key moments.

When choosing a photographer or videographer, it's important to ask the right questions to ensure you're hiring a professional who matches your vision and expectations. Start by asking about the type of cameras and lenses they use. High-quality gear doesn't automatically make someone a great photographer, but it's a good indicator of their commitment to delivering professional results.

Also, ask if they utilize off-camera or on-camera flash photography. This is especially important for weddings held in dimly lit venues, where proper lighting can make or break your photos and videos. A skilled professional will know how to balance natural light with artificial lighting to create flattering, well-lit images.

One of the most crucial questions to ask is whether they themselves will be the one photographing or filming your wedding. If they hesitate, provide a vague response, or dodge the question, this could be a red flag. Often, this indicates you're dealing with an agency that outsources work to low-paid, less experienced freelancers. This kind of bait-and-switch practice is unfortunately common in the wedding industry. While agencies can still deliver good results if they work with skilled professionals, the risk is higher that you'll end up with an amateur who doesn't meet your expectations.

Additional Questions to Ask

To help avoid unpleasant surprises, ask these additional questions:

1. **Experience and Style**
   - How many weddings have you personally photographed or filmed?
   - Can you show me a full wedding gallery or video from a real event?
   - What is your approach—candid, posed, artistic, or a mix of styles?
2. **Team and Coverage**
   - Do you work with a second shooter or assistant or offer one for an additional price?
   - How many hours of coverage does your package include?
   - Will you stay longer if the wedding runs late? What are the additional costs?
3. **Logistics and Deliverables**
   - How long will it take to receive our edited photos/videos?
   - How many edited photos or hours of footage can we expect?
   - Do you provide high-resolution digital files, prints, or albums?
4. **Backup and Contingency Plans**
   - What happens if you're unable to make it to the wedding?
   - Do you bring backup equipment in case of technical issues?
5. **Contracts and Policies**
   - Can I see a sample contract?
   - What is your cancellation policy?
   - Do you carry liability insurance (important for venues that require it)?

Red Flags to Watch Out For

- **Canned Responses:** If their answers feel rehearsed or generic, they may not have a genuine passion for the craft or a clear understanding of your specific needs.
- **Unclear Portfolios:** If they can't show you a portfolio with real weddings, or only provide heavily edited staged shoots, this could mean a lack of real-world experience.
- **Vague Pricing:** If their pricing structure isn't transparent, they might be hiding hidden fees or upselling aggressively.
- **No Contract:** Always insist on a signed agreement to protect both parties and clarify expectations.

Hiring the right photographer or videographer is about more than just skill—it's about trust and communication. Take the time to thoroughly vet your options, and don't hesitate to walk away if something doesn't feel right. After all, this person will be responsible for capturing the memories you'll cherish for a lifetime.

- Check reviews and testimonials to assess whether a vendor is reliable and professional. Be cautious, as some vendors may post fake reviews to boost their reputation, while others may lack reviews simply because they don't routinely ask clients to leave feedback (many satisfied customers don't leave reviews unless prompted due to busy schedules). Trust your gut during your interactions. Do they come across as honest, authentic, and down-to-earth? Do they answer your questions clearly and confidently? Or do they seem like a pushy salesperson who dodges questions by deflecting or turning them into questions? If it's the latter, trust your instincts and move on. The right vendor will make you feel comfortable, heard, and confident in their ability to deliver. That said, don't let one bad review scare you off. There are always a few unreasonable people in the world, and even shady competitors who post fake negative reviews to manipulate algorithms. Nearly every vendor has encountered these challenges. Instead, focus on the overall pattern of reviews and pay attention to how the vendor responds to negative feedback. Their response can often reveal more about their professionalism and reliability than the review itself.

3. **Personality and Compatibility**
    - Speak with them before booking, ideally with a phone call. Since you'll spend a lot of time with your photographer or videographer on your wedding day, it's essential to feel comfortable with them. If you're on a tighter budget, a phone call is sufficient and respectful of their time—many photographers live in more affordable rural areas and may need to drive several hours to reach venues in larger cities. However, if you're investing more than $3,000 in photography, consider asking them to meet you at the venue to review everything in person before signing the contract. Otherwise, a phone call will usually suffice but is still optional. In my experience, only about 50% of clients feel the need to talk directly—most are comfortable booking after exchanging a few emails, reviewing the website, and checking testimonials or reviews.
    - Look for someone who listens to your ideas and understands your priorities.

4. **Packages and Pricing**
    - Ensure the package fits your budget and includes what you need (hours of coverage, number of edited photos, or length of the final video).
    - Ask about add-ons, such as second shooters, drone footage, or highlight reels.
    - Be clear on what's included: Are travel costs, prints, or albums part of the package?

5. **Technical Skills and Equipment**
    - Confirm they use high-quality cameras and equipment. For videographers, ask about sound recording capabilities.

- Ensure they have a plan for backups—both for their equipment and your files.

Must-Have Shots and Video Moments

Pre-Ceremony

- **Candid Morning Moments:**
    - Bride and bridesmaids toasting with champagne or coffee.
    - Groom and groomsmen sharing a laugh, adjusting ties, or cufflinks.
    - Final touches, such as the bride putting on earrings or veil.
- **Meaningful Details:**
    - Close-ups of heirloom items, like jewelry, a pocket watch, or handkerchiefs.
    - A shot of the bouquet with handwritten vows or invitations.
    - Rings in creative settings, like atop flowers, books, or sentimental objects.
- **Personal First Looks:**
    - Bride's first look with her father, mother, or siblings.
    - Groom's first look with his parents or groomsmen.
    - Couple reading letters or notes they wrote to each other.

Ceremony

- **Unique Perspectives:**
    - Wide-angle shot of the entire ceremony setup before guests arrive.
    - Guests' reactions as the processional begins (especially parents or grandparents).
    - Over-the-shoulder shot of the bride walking down the aisle from her perspective.
    - Close-ups of hands during the ring exchange.
- **Special Traditions:**
    - Religious or cultural rituals (lighting a unity candle, breaking the glass, jumping the broom, etc.).
    - Signing of marriage documents or certificate (if part of the ceremony).
- **Memorable Exit:**
    - Confetti, flower petals, bubbles, or sparklers as the couple walks back down the aisle.

Portraits and Group Photos

- **Couple Portraits:**
    - Silhouettes at sunset or against dramatic backdrops.

- - Romantic shots with long veils or flowing trains in motion.
  - Close-ups of hands with rings, bouquet, or intertwined fingers.
  - Creative framing with natural elements like arches, windows, or trees.
- **Bridal Party Fun:**
  - Bridesmaids fluffing the bride's dress or veil.
  - Groomsmen laughing or striking humorous poses.
  - Full wedding party jumping or celebrating together.
- **Family Poses:**
  - Generational photos (e.g., bride/groom with grandparents).
  - Candid family interactions, like hugs or shared laughs.

Reception

- **Details and Decor:**
  - Close-ups of the menu cards, place settings, and guest favors.
  - Full table and room shots before guests arrive.
  - Lighting elements like candles, chandeliers, or fairy lights.
- **Key Moments:**
  - Couple's reactions during speeches and toasts.
  - Kids playing or dancing during the reception.
  - Guests interacting at photo booths or activity stations.
- **Unique Reception Moments:**
  - Crowd reactions during a surprise dance or performance.
  - Groom removing and tossing the garter.
  - Couple sharing a quiet moment together away from the crowd.

Post-Wedding and Send-Off

- **Memorable Farewells:**
  - The couple's grand exit with sparklers, lanterns, or a vintage car getaway.
  - Guests waving goodbye with signs, ribbons, or bubbles.
- **After-Party Fun:**
  - Photos of the late-night crowd (especially if outfits or vibes have shifted).
  - Fun shots of the bride or groom joining friends on the dance floor.

For Videographers

- **Voiceover Material:**
    - Recording the bride or groom reading vows or letters (can be edited into the final video).
    - Audio snippets of guests sharing well wishes.
- **Behind-the-Scenes Moments:**
    - Footage of the couple getting ready, laughing with their wedding party, or practicing vows.
    - Pre-ceremony guest arrival and mingling.
- **Unique Storytelling Shots:**
    - Time-lapses of venue setup or sunset transitions.
    - Drone footage capturing the venue's surroundings (if allowed).

For weddings with larger budgets, some couples choose to create staged, cinematic scenes filmed on a day prior to their wedding. For example, the bride might be filmed opening and reading a heartfelt love letter from the groom, interspersed with moments that tell their story—such as how they first met, got engaged, and other milestones in their relationship. Some videos might have them swimming in a pool in slow motion, while the one reads the letter in a very cinematic fashion. These videos often incorporate photos or old footage, which can now even be enhanced using AI video generators to bring still images to life as if they were filmed.

Producing these "film-style" videos requires additional time and resources. Expect to spend an entire day filming and budget at least $1,500 on top of your wedding videography package. You'll also need to organize and provide content for the videographer or editor, such as photos, recorded messages, or specific details you'd like included.

Many couples showcase these videos during the reception, projecting them on a big screen or projector for guests to enjoy. They're a beautiful way to personalize the day, share your love story, and entertain your guests. However, it's important to plan and communicate clearly with your videographer to ensure the production aligns with your vision and timeline. If you don't have the budget, but want to make a video like this; you could always turn a date night into a DIY film set using smartphones, and then AI tools such as Runway or Kling AI while editing to make it look like a Hollywood movie.

If you don't have the budget for a professionally produced wedding video like this, you can still create something magical by turning a date night into a DIY film set. With a little creativity, you can use smartphones to shoot your footage and then enhance it with AI tools like **Runway** or **Kling AI** during the editing process to give it a polished, Hollywood-style look.

Tips for a DIY Wedding Video on a Budget:

1. **Plan Your Shots**
    - Outline a simple storyboard of key moments to film, such as reading love letters, recreating your first date, or sharing your favorite memories.

- Scout a location with good lighting and minimal background noise—sunset hours or softly lit indoor settings work great.

2. **Maximize Your Smartphone's Capabilities**
    - Use a smartphone with high-resolution video capabilities (4K if possible).
    - Stabilize your shots with a tripod or gimbal to avoid shaky footage.
    - Experiment with slow-motion or time-lapse settings for added drama.

3. **Use DIY Lighting**
    - Grab inexpensive LED lights or desk lamps to create soft, flattering lighting.
    - For evening shots, use candles or fairy lights for a warm, romantic glow.

4. **Enhance with AI Tools**
    - **Runway:** Add cinematic effects, color grading, or AI-powered enhancements to give your video a professional edge.
    - **Kling AI:** Use AI to smooth transitions, create overlays, or add special effects.
    - AI upscaling tools can also improve the quality of your smartphone footage, making it look like it was shot on higher-end equipment.

5. **Edit Like a Pro**
    - Free editing software like **DaVinci Resolve** or **CapCut** can help you piece your footage together seamlessly.
    - Incorporate music that's meaningful to you as a couple, or search for royalty-free tracks online for emotional backing.

6. **Add Personal Touches**
    - Include scanned photos, handwritten notes, or snippets of your favorite songs.
    - Record voiceovers to narrate your love story or describe the moments that mean the most to you.

7. **Present It Creatively**
    - Share your finished video during your reception on a projector or screen.
    - Alternatively, upload it to your wedding website for friends and family to view before or after the big day.

With a little effort and creativity, a DIY wedding video can be just as meaningful as a professional one—and the process of creating it together can become a cherished memory in itself.

Custom Moments Based on Your Story

- Include anything unique to your relationship or theme, such as:
    - Pets incorporated into the ceremony or portraits.

- A choreographed first dance or flash mob involving the bridal party.
- Reaction shots during surprise gifts or speeches.

Pro Tip: Creating Your Shot List

- **Collaborate with Your Photographer/Videographer:** Share a detailed shot list of your must-haves but allow flexibility for candid moments and creative input.
- **Assign a Helper:** Designate someone who knows your family and friends to assist in gathering people for group photos. This keeps things efficient and avoids missing important shots.

Customizable Wedding Photography & Videography Shot List Template

Here's a shot list template you can provide to your photographer and videographer to ensure no important moments are missed. It covers pre-wedding, ceremony, and reception, with room for customization.

1. Pre-Ceremony

- Bride getting ready (hair, makeup, putting on the dress).
- Groom getting ready (adjusting tie, cufflinks, putting on jacket).
- Close-ups of:
    - Dress on hanger.
    - Shoes, jewelry, and accessories.
    - Bouquet and boutonnières.
- Bride with bridesmaids (laughing, toasting, helping with the dress).
- Groom with groomsmen (fixing ties, casual group shot).
- First look moments:
    - Bride with father/mother.
    - Bride and groom.

2. Ceremony

- Exterior and interior shots of the venue before guests arrive.
- Guests arriving and mingling.
- Processional moments:
    - Wedding party walking down the aisle.

- Bride walking down the aisle (wide-angle and close-up).
- Groom's reaction.
- Key ceremony moments:
    - Exchanging vows.
    - Exchanging rings.
    - First kiss.
- Recessional (couple exiting the ceremony, confetti, or bubbles).
- Candid guest reactions during the ceremony.

---

3. Portraits

Couple Portraits

- Romantic close-ups of the couple.
- Full-length shots of the couple with the venue backdrop.
- Creative shots with props (veil, bouquet, or unique decor elements).
- Candid moments of the couple interacting (laughing, walking, or sharing a kiss).

Bridal Party

- Entire bridal party (formal and fun poses).
- Bride with bridesmaids.
- Groom with groomsmen.
- Candid group interactions (toasts, cheers, or laughs).

Family Portraits

- Bride and groom with:
    - Parents (both sets).
    - Immediate family (siblings, grandparents).
    - Extended family (aunts, uncles, cousins).
- Individual shots of bride/groom with parents.

---

4. Reception

Details and Decor

- Venue decor before guests arrive (tables, centerpieces, cake, lighting).

- Wedding favors, guestbook, and seating chart.

Grand Entrance and First Dance

- Couple's grand entrance.
- First dance (wide-angle and close-up).
- Parent dances (bride with father, groom with mother).

Key Events

- Toasts and speeches (capture reactions from both speakers and the couple).
- Cake cutting.
- Bouquet toss or garter toss.
- Special traditions (cultural dances, games, or rituals).

Candid Moments

- Guests dancing and celebrating.
- Kids having fun.
- Candid interactions (laughter, hugs, and toasts).

---

5. Send-Off and Post-Wedding

- Couple's grand exit (sparklers, confetti, bubbles, or car getaway).
- Wide-angle shot of the venue lit up at night.
- Post-wedding moments:
    - Quiet, intimate moments of the couple.
    - Group photo of late-night revelers.

Pro Tips for Couples Using This Shot List

1. **Personalize It:** Add any special moments or traditions unique to your wedding.
2. **Designate a Helper:** Assign a trusted friend or family member to help coordinate group shots.
3. **Share It Early:** Provide your photographer/videographer with this list during your initial meeting or consultation.
4. **Prioritize:** Highlight or number your top priorities so your team knows what's most important.

Hiring Vendors

Your vendors play a vital role in making your wedding day seamless and memorable. Choosing the right caterers, bakers, DJs or bands, and officiants involves more than just booking someone who fits your budget—it's about finding professionals whose style, personality, and skills align with your vision. This section will guide you through selecting the right vendors, handling contracts, maintaining clear communication, and setting realistic expectations.

How to Choose Vendors

1. **Caterers**
   - **Taste Tests:** Schedule a tasting to sample their menu and ensure their food aligns with your preferences.
   - **Customization:** Ask if they can accommodate dietary restrictions or create custom dishes.
   - **Experience:** Choose a caterer familiar with your venue or one experienced in similar-sized events.
   - **Service Style:** Determine whether you want a plated dinner, buffet, or family-style service.
2. **Bakers**
   - **Portfolio Review:** Look through their previous wedding cakes to evaluate their design capabilities.
   - **Tastings:** Sample cake flavors and fillings to ensure they match your taste and theme.
   - **Customization:** Confirm if they can replicate your desired design or create a custom style.
   - **Delivery Details:** Ensure they handle delivery and setup on the wedding day.
3. **DJs/Bands**
   - **Style Compatibility:** Discuss their style and playlist options to ensure they can match your musical preferences.
   - **Energy Management:** A great DJ or band can read the room and adjust music to keep the energy up. Ask for examples of how they've done this at other events.
   - **Equipment:** Confirm they provide their own sound system, microphones, and lighting if needed.
   - **References:** Request reviews or videos of past performances to assess their professionalism and style.
4. **Officiants**
   - **Experience and Tone:** Choose someone whose personality and approach align with the type of ceremony you envision—formal, spiritual, or casual.
   - **Customization:** Ask if they're willing to personalize the ceremony by incorporating your love story, cultural traditions, or custom vows.

- **Legal Requirements:** Verify that they're legally authorized to officiate in your location and can handle any necessary paperwork.

Contracts, Communication, and Managing Expectations

1. **Contracts**
   - **Read Carefully:** Ensure all details are included, such as services provided, hours of coverage, pricing, and cancellation/refund policies.
   - **Payment Schedule:** Confirm the deposit amount, due dates, and final payment deadline.
   - **Contingency Plans:** Check for clauses covering emergencies, such as vendor illness or equipment failure.
2. **Communication**
   - **Be Specific:** Provide detailed instructions about your vision and expectations. Share mood boards, song lists, or specific requests to ensure clarity.
   - **Point of Contact:** Designate a trusted person (like your planner or a member of the wedding party) to liaise with vendors on the day of the wedding.
   - **Follow-Up:** Keep a timeline for checking in with vendors as the wedding day approaches to confirm details and logistics.
3. **Managing Expectations**
   - **Budget vs. Vision:** Be realistic about what's possible within your budget. Communicate priorities so vendors know where to focus their efforts.
   - **Trust the Professionals:** While you should clearly communicate your preferences, trust vendors to use their expertise to make decisions.
   - **Flexibility:** Be prepared for minor adjustments—unexpected issues like weather changes or delays can sometimes require quick thinking and collaboration.

Final Tip: Build a Strong Team

Treat your vendors as part of your wedding team. By maintaining clear, respectful communication and setting expectations upfront, you'll create an environment where they can do their best work, ensuring your day is everything you've dreamed of.

Vendor-Specific Questions

Caterers

- Do you offer customizable menus?

- Can you accommodate dietary restrictions (vegetarian, vegan, gluten-free, etc.)?
- What is your service style (buffet, plated, family-style)?
- What does your pricing include (servers, cleanup, tableware, linens)?
- Are there additional fees for travel, overtime, or special requests?
- Can we do a tasting before finalizing the menu?

Bakers

- Do you offer tastings, and is there a fee for them?
- Can you create a custom cake design or replicate one we like?
- How far in advance is the cake prepared?
- How do you handle delivery and setup on the wedding day?
- Do you provide cake stands or cutting utensils?
- Can you accommodate dietary restrictions (allergies, gluten-free, etc.)?

DJs/Bands

- What is your style and approach to creating a playlist?
- Are you open to requests from the couple and guests?
- Do you provide your own equipment (sound system, microphones, lighting)?
- Have you worked at our venue before?
- What do you do if equipment fails or there are technical difficulties?
- How do you handle transitions between songs or speeches?
- Do you have videos of past performances or references?

Officiants

- How long have you been officiating weddings?
- Do you offer pre-marital counseling or meetings to get to know us better?
- Are you open to incorporating personal touches, such as custom vows, readings, or cultural traditions?
- Do you provide a script or outline of the ceremony in advance?
- Will you handle the legal paperwork and submission of the marriage license?
- Do you require a rehearsal?

Key Contract Elements

When reviewing a contract, look for the following details to protect yourself and set clear expectations:

1. **Service Details**

- A complete list of services the vendor will provide (e.g., "DJ will play for 5 hours," "Caterer will serve a buffet for 150 guests").
- Specific start and end times for their services.
- Items included (e.g., linens, lighting equipment, backup generators).

2. **Pricing and Payment Terms**
   - Total cost of services, with a detailed breakdown of fees (e.g., deposit, balance, travel fees, overtime charges).
   - Payment schedule, including due dates for deposits and final payments.
   - Refund and cancellation policies, including any non-refundable deposits.

3. **Contingency Plans**
   - What happens if the vendor cannot perform due to illness, equipment failure, or other emergencies?
   - Who is responsible for finding a replacement?
   - Backup options for outdoor services in case of inclement weather.

4. **Timing and Delivery**
   - For caterers and bakers: Delivery times for food and setup details.
   - For DJs/bands: Arrival time for setup and sound checks.
   - For photographers/videographers: Turnaround time for edited photos or videos.

5. **Liability and Insurance**
   - Proof of liability insurance, especially if required by the venue.
   - A statement clarifying who is responsible for damages or injuries caused by the vendor.

6. **Ownership of Deliverables** (for photographers/videographers)
   - Who owns the rights to the photos or videos?
   - Whether you'll receive high-resolution files, prints, or both.
   - Terms for sharing or using photos/videos on social media or portfolios.

Pro Tips for Contracts and Vendor Management

1. **Always Get It in Writing:** Verbal agreements are not enough. A detailed, signed contract protects both you and the vendor.
2. **Negotiate Where Possible:** Ask if there's flexibility in pricing or services. For example, a caterer might waive a delivery fee if your venue is nearby.
3. **Follow Up:** Once the contract is signed, schedule a follow-up meeting or email closer to the wedding date to confirm details and address last-minute updates.

Part 4: Bringing It All Together

With your plans in place and your dream team assembled, it's time to focus on the finer details that will bring your wedding day to life. This is where all the pieces come together—creating a seamless flow, ensuring everything runs smoothly, and making sure your big day feels as special as you've envisioned. From structuring your ceremony to planning the perfect reception and building a day-of timeline, this section will help you tie up loose ends and enjoy the celebration without unnecessary stress.

What to Expect in This Section

1. **Planning the Ceremony**
   - Designing the structure: from the processional to the recessional.
   - Incorporating meaningful rituals, readings, or traditions.
2. **Organizing the Reception**
   - Setting the schedule: speeches, dances, and entertainment.
   - Tips for creating an enjoyable atmosphere for guests.
3. **Creating a Day-of Timeline**
   - Building a timeline to keep the day running smoothly.
   - Key tips for handling last-minute surprises.

This part of the book will focus on making your wedding day unforgettable by ensuring all the details work in harmony. Let's start with planning the most meaningful part of your day—the ceremony.

Planning the Ceremony

Your ceremony is the heart of your wedding day—it's the moment you make your promises and begin your life together. Designing the flow of your ceremony is about more than just timing; it's about creating a meaningful and personal experience that reflects your love story. This section will help you plan the details, from vows and rituals to music and traditions, while offering tips for working with your officiant and adding personal touches.

Designing the Flow

1. **Processional**
   - Decide on the order of the processional. Commonly:
     - Officiant.

- Groom and groomsmen (or groom enters solo).
- Bridesmaids.
- Flower girl/ring bearer.
- Bride (traditionally accompanied by a parent or guardian).
  - Choose music that sets the tone for the event, whether it's classical, modern, or something personal to you both.

2. **Welcome and Opening Remarks**
   - The officiant welcomes guests and sets the tone for the ceremony. This is often a mix of formal greetings, personal anecdotes, and warm remarks about love and commitment.

3. **Vows**
   - Decide whether to write your own vows or use traditional ones.
   - For personal vows, focus on what makes your partner special, promises for the future, and the meaning of your relationship.
   - Practice your vows ahead of time to feel confident delivering them.

4. **Rituals and Traditions**
   - Incorporate meaningful rituals, such as:
     - Unity ceremonies (e.g., lighting a candle, mixing sand, or tying a knot).
     - Religious or cultural traditions (e.g., breaking the glass, jumping the broom, or handfasting).
     - Modern twists, such as a wine blending or planting a tree together.
   - Keep rituals concise to maintain the flow of the ceremony.

5. **Readings**
   - Choose readings that resonate with you as a couple. These can be:
     - Religious texts, poems, or literary excerpts.
     - Quotes from favorite authors, movies, or songs.
     - Personal letters or meaningful words written by friends or family.

6. **Exchange of Rings**
   - Rings are exchanged along with meaningful words, either traditional or written by you.
   - Practice ahead of time to avoid fumbling with rings on the big day.

7. **Pronouncement and First Kiss**
   - The officiant announces you as a married couple, followed by the first kiss.
   - Discuss with your officiant if you'd like them to phrase this in a specific way.

8. **Recessional**
   - Choose upbeat music for your exit as a married couple.
   - Consider including fun elements, such as tossing petals, confetti, or bubbles as you walk back down the aisle.

Tips for Working with Officiants and Including Personal Touches

1. **Working with Officiants**
    - **Choose Someone Who Matches Your Vision:** Whether they're a religious leader, a secular officiant, or a close friend, your officiant should align with the tone and style of your ceremony.
    - **Share Your Story:** Meet with your officiant beforehand to discuss your relationship and what you'd like them to include in their remarks.
    - **Review the Script:** Ask for a draft of the ceremony script so you can suggest edits or additions.
    - **Rehearse Together:** If possible, include your officiant in the rehearsal to ensure everything flows smoothly.
2. **Adding Personal Touches**
    - **Personalized Vows:** Writing your own vows adds a unique and heartfelt element to the ceremony.
    - **Include Family or Friends:** Ask loved ones to participate by reading, playing music, or sharing a few words during the ceremony.
    - **Symbolic Items:** Incorporate objects with sentimental value, such as a family heirloom or a special keepsake, into your ceremony decor or rituals.
    - **Surprise Elements:** Surprise your partner with a special reading, a song, or a gesture that holds personal meaning for both of you.

Final Tip: Make It Yours

Remember, there's no "right" way to plan a ceremony—it's about what feels meaningful to you as a couple. Whether your style is traditional, modern, or somewhere in between, focus on creating a ceremony that celebrates your love and reflects your journey together.

Organizing the Reception

The reception is your chance to celebrate with friends and family, creating a lively, memorable atmosphere for everyone. Whether you're planning a formal dinner or a relaxed party, a well-organized schedule and thoughtful activities will ensure your guests have a great time. This section focuses on structuring the reception and adding unique elements that will surprise and delight your guests.

Setting the Schedule

A clear schedule keeps your reception running smoothly, ensuring guests are entertained and key moments are captured. Here's a typical timeline to guide you:

1. **Grand Entrance**
   - The couple makes a dramatic entrance, often accompanied by the wedding party.
   - Choose upbeat music that reflects your personality as a couple.
2. **First Dance**
   - Kick off the celebration with your first dance as a married couple. This is often followed by parent dances (e.g., bride and father, groom and mother).
3. **Dinner Service**
   - Whether you're having a buffet, plated dinner, or family-style meal, allow 45–60 minutes for guests to eat.
   - Play background music to create a relaxed atmosphere.
4. **Toasts and Speeches**
   - Traditionally, the best man and maid of honor give speeches, followed by parents or close family members.
   - Keep speeches brief (3–5 minutes each) to maintain energy and avoid losing guest attention.
5. **Cake Cutting**
   - A symbolic moment that can be scheduled after dinner or later in the evening.
   - Use this time to invite guests to enjoy dessert or coffee.
6. **Dancing and Entertainment**
   - Open the dance floor with a high-energy song after the formalities.
   - Alternate between slow songs and upbeat tracks to cater to all guests.
7. **Special Traditions or Activities**
   - Include bouquet and garter tosses, cultural dances, or games as part of the festivities.
   - Plan these events earlier in the evening if you want to keep the energy high.
8. **Grand Exit**
   - End the night with a memorable send-off, such as a sparkler exit, confetti toss, or lantern release.

Ideas for Activities and Surprises That Guests Will Love

1. **Interactive Guest Experiences**
   - **Photo Booths:** Provide props and a fun backdrop for guests to take photos.
   - **DIY Stations:** Set up a guestbook table, where guests can leave Polaroids or write messages on small cards.
   - **Custom Drink Stations:** Offer a build-your-own cocktail or mocktail bar.
2. **Unique Entertainment**

- **Live Performances:** Hire a band, string quartet, or even a surprise act like a magician or caricature artist.
- **Cultural Showcases:** Include a traditional dance, drum performance, or other cultural elements unique to you and your partner.
- **Games:** Lawn games like cornhole, giant Jenga, or trivia about the couple can keep guests entertained during quieter moments.

3. **Surprise Elements**
   - **Late-Night Snacks:** Treat guests to unexpected comfort food like mini burgers, pizza slices, or donuts as the night winds down.
   - **Fireworks Display:** If your venue allows it, a fireworks finale can wow your guests and create a magical ending.
   - **Special Performances:** Surprise guests with a choreographed first dance or a flash mob involving the wedding party.

4. **Kids' Activities**
   - Create a dedicated kids' area with coloring books, toys, or movies to keep younger guests entertained.

5. **Thank-You Moments**
   - Give a heartfelt toast or play a video thanking your guests for being part of your special day.
   - Provide personalized favors, such as handwritten notes or small keepsakes, to make each guest feel appreciated.

Final Tip: Keep It Fun and Flexible

While it's important to have a schedule, don't be afraid to adapt as the night unfolds. If guests are enjoying a particular activity or dancing the night away, let the celebration flow naturally. A well-organized reception ensures everyone feels included and leaves with lasting memories of your special day.

Additional Ideas for Surprises and Enhancing Guest Engagement

Here are more creative ways to elevate your reception and keep your guests engaged throughout the celebration:

Interactive and Personalized Experiences

1. **Live Artist or Painter**
   - Hire an artist to create a live painting of the ceremony or reception as it happens. Guests will love watching the artwork come to life, and it makes for a stunning keepsake.
2. **Message Tree or Wish Jar**

- Set up a tree or a beautiful jar where guests can leave notes, advice, or wishes for the couple.
- Provide prompts or pre-cut cards to make it easier for guests to participate.

3. **Custom Photo Experiences**
   - Rent a 360-degree photo booth or slow-motion video booth for a high-tech twist on the classic photo booth.
   - Offer printed photos as keepsakes or digital versions guests can instantly share.
4. **Signature Drink Naming Contest**
   - Have a menu of drinks but let guests vote on names for your signature cocktails. The winning names can be announced by the DJ during the reception.
5. **Interactive Food Stations**
   - Create stations where guests can customize their meals or desserts, such as:
     - A taco or pasta bar.
     - A DIY s'mores station.
     - A waffle or ice cream sundae bar.

Surprise Performances

1. **Cultural or Themed Dances**
   - Include a cultural performance or a choreographed routine (e.g., a traditional Haka, a Bollywood dance, or a flamenco show).
2. **Groom or Bride Performance**
   - Surprise your partner and guests with a solo performance, such as singing your favorite song or playing an instrument.
3. **Flash Mob or Wedding Party Dance**
   - Secretly plan a group dance with your wedding party to surprise the crowd.

Engaging Guest Activities

1. **Table Trivia or Icebreakers**
   - Place trivia cards about the couple on each table to spark conversation. Include funny, romantic, or unexpected facts to keep guests entertained.
2. **Memory Jar or Wall**
   - Ask guests to write down their favorite memories of you as a couple and post them on a wall or drop them into a jar.
3. **Silent Disco**
   - Rent headphones for a silent disco, where guests can choose from multiple music channels. It's a unique, fun way to keep the dance floor alive.

Late-Night Surprises

1. **Midnight Snack Stations**
    - Delight guests with a snack station featuring mini sliders, fries, popcorn, or even breakfast items like waffles or mini pancakes.
2. **Custom Dessert Bar**
    - Offer a variety of desserts that tie into your theme, such as macaron towers, mini cupcakes, or gourmet donuts.
3. **Glow-in-the-Dark Fun**
    - Hand out glow sticks, LED glasses, or light-up bracelets for an after-dark dance party.

Wow-Worthy Endings

1. **Surprise Send-Offs**
    - Plan a dramatic exit with unique touches, such as:
        - A sparkler tunnel.
        - A vintage car or horse-drawn carriage.
        - Floating lanterns or confetti cannons.
2. **Firework or Drone Show**
    - If your venue allows it, end the night with a small fireworks display or a coordinated drone light show.
3. **Custom Thank-You Gifts**
    - Hand out personalized gifts as guests leave, such as mini bottles of champagne, potted succulents, or handmade candles.

Final Thought: Include Moments Unique to You

The best surprises and activities are those that reflect your personality as a couple. Whether it's a shared hobby, cultural tradition, or a quirky idea you've always dreamed of, these touches will make your reception unforgettable for you and your guests.

Creating a Day-of Timeline

A well-planned day-of timeline is essential for ensuring your wedding runs smoothly. It helps everyone—vendors, wedding party, and even you—know where to be and when, minimizing stress and confusion. This section includes sample schedules for different types of weddings and tips for handling last-minute emergencies like a pro.

Sample Schedules for Smooth Transitions

Here are examples of typical wedding day timelines based on ceremony time. Adjust them to fit your specific needs and preferences.

Sample Timeline for a 4:00 PM Ceremony

8:00 AM – 10:00 AM: Getting Ready

- Hair and makeup for the bride and bridal party begins.
- Groom and groomsmen start getting ready.
- Photographer arrives for detail shots (dress, rings, bouquet) and candid moments.

10:00 AM – 12:00 PM: Final Touches

- Bride and bridesmaids finish hair and makeup.
- Groomsmen dress and take casual group photos.

12:00 PM – 1:30 PM: First Look & Portraits

- First look between bride and groom.
- Couple's portraits and group photos with bridal party and family.

1:30 PM – 3:30 PM: Venue Setup & Break Time

- Vendors finalize decor, seating, and floral arrangements at the ceremony and reception sites.
- Couple and wedding party take a quick break to relax and hydrate.

4:00 PM – 4:30 PM: Ceremony

- Guests arrive 30 minutes prior and are seated.
- Ceremony begins and lasts approximately 20–30 minutes.

4:30 PM – 5:00 PM: Post-Ceremony Photos

- Quick group photos with family and wedding party.

5:00 PM – 6:00 PM: Cocktail Hour

- Guests mingle, enjoy appetizers and drinks, and sign the guestbook.
- Couple takes a few candid shots and joins the tail end of cocktail hour.

6:00 PM – 10:00 PM: Reception

- 6:00 PM: Grand entrance and first dance.
- 6:15 PM: Dinner service begins.
- 7:00 PM: Speeches and toasts.
- 7:30 PM: Parent dances and open dance floor.
- 9:00 PM: Cake cutting and late-night snacks.
- 10:00 PM: Grand exit (sparklers, confetti, or getaway car).

Key Tips for Timeline Adjustments

- **Morning Weddings:** Shift everything earlier. Brunch weddings typically wrap up by 2:00 PM.
- **Evening Weddings:** Start later but allow extra time for lighting adjustments, especially if the ceremony is outdoors at sunset.
- **Cultural or Religious Ceremonies:** Factor in time for specific rituals or traditions.

Handling Last-Minute Emergencies

No matter how well you plan, unexpected issues can arise. Here's how to stay calm and keep your wedding on track:

1. **Common Emergencies and Quick Fixes**
   - **Vendor Delays:** Have backup contact numbers for all vendors. Assign a trusted person to follow up and handle coordination.
   - **Weather Changes:** Ensure your venue has an indoor or covered option for outdoor weddings. Stock up on umbrellas or portable fans as needed.
   - **Wardrobe Malfunctions:** Keep a wedding day emergency kit on hand with safety pins, sewing kits, fashion tape, and stain remover.
   - **Timing Delays:** Pad your timeline with 15–30-minute buffers between major events to account for minor delays.
2. **Assign Roles**
   - **Day-of Coordinator:** If you don't have a planner, assign someone reliable to oversee the schedule and manage vendor arrivals.

-
  - **Point Person for Emergencies:** Choose a calm, organized person (not you!) to handle last-minute issues.
3. **Communicate Changes Quickly**
    - If changes arise, let your vendors and wedding party know immediately. Text or group chats are great for quick updates.
4. **Stay Flexible**
    - Remember, your guests likely won't notice if the day doesn't go exactly as planned. Focus on enjoying the moments that matter most.

Final Tip: Pad Your Schedule

Adding extra time throughout your timeline for transitions, unexpected delays, or breaks will help you stay relaxed and on track. A well-planned timeline not only ensures a smooth day but also gives you more time to enjoy your wedding without feeling rushed.

Part 5: Pre- and Post-Wedding Essentials

Your wedding day is just one part of the journey. The lead-up and the aftermath are just as important to ensuring the overall experience is smooth, stress-free, and memorable. This section covers the essentials for handling pre-wedding tasks and post-wedding responsibilities, so nothing gets overlooked.

What to Expect in This Section

1. **Pre-Wedding Tasks**
    - Finalizing details with vendors.
    - Preparing an emergency kit.
    - Handling rehearsal dinners and pre-wedding events.
2. **Post-Wedding Responsibilities**
    - Returning rentals and collecting belongings.
    - Sending thank-you notes.
    - Preserving your dress and storing keepsakes.
    - Legal tasks: name changes, updating documents, and more.

Planning and celebrating your wedding doesn't end when the party's over. Let's start by tackling the tasks that lead up to the big day, so you're fully prepared for your celebration.

Pre-Wedding Events

Pre-wedding events are an opportunity to celebrate your upcoming marriage with family and friends while setting the tone for the big day. Whether you're planning engagement parties, bridal showers, or bachelor/bachelorette parties, or organizing a memorable rehearsal dinner, this section will help you manage these celebrations with ease.

Planning Engagement Parties

1. **Purpose:**
    - An engagement party is the first celebration after saying "yes," giving you a chance to share the joy with loved ones.
    - Typically hosted by the couple, parents, or close friends.
2. **Planning Tips:**

- **Timing:** Host the party within 1–3 months of your engagement.
- **Guest List:** Keep it small and intimate, inviting close family and friends.
- **Venue:** Options range from someone's home to restaurants, backyards, or even parks for a casual vibe.
- **Activities:** Consider speeches, toasts, or simple games to make it interactive.

Planning Bridal Showers

1. **Purpose:**
   - A bridal shower is a gift-giving party traditionally hosted by the maid of honor, bridesmaids, or family.
   - It's a chance for loved ones to support the bride and shower her with good wishes.
2. **Planning Tips:**
   - **Timing:** Host the shower 1–3 months before the wedding.
   - **Guest List:** Close family, friends, and wedding party members are typically invited.
   - **Theme:** Choose a theme that reflects the bride's personality (e.g., tea party, garden brunch, or travel-inspired).
   - **Activities:** Incorporate games, gift-opening moments, or a toast to honor the bride.

Bachelor/Bachelorette Parties

1. **Purpose:**
   - These parties are a fun, often playful way to celebrate with close friends before the wedding day.
2. **Planning Tips:**
   - **Timing:** Plan for a few weeks to a month before the wedding to avoid pre-wedding stress or exhaustion.
   - **Guest List:** Keep it to close friends and wedding party members.
   - **Activities:**
     - Traditional: Night out on the town, dinner, and dancing.
     - Low-Key: Spa day, wine tasting, or a relaxing weekend getaway.
     - Adventurous: Camping, hiking, or other outdoor activities.
   - **Budget:** Be mindful of guests' budgets and choose activities that everyone can enjoy comfortably.

Rehearsal Dinner Tips and Etiquette

1. **Purpose:**
    - The rehearsal dinner is a relaxed gathering the evening before the wedding, often following the ceremony rehearsal.
    - It allows the couple and their families to connect, thank the wedding party, and kick off the celebration.
2. **Planning Tips:**
    - **Who Hosts:** Traditionally, the groom's family hosts, but modern etiquette allows for the couple or both families to co-host.
    - **Guest List:** Include immediate family, the wedding party, and anyone involved in the ceremony (officiant, readers, etc.). You can also invite out-of-town guests as a courtesy.
    - **Venue:** Choose a relaxed setting, such as a restaurant, family home, or outdoor space.
    - **Schedule:**
        - Welcome toast by the host.
        - Optional speeches by parents, the couple, or close friends.
        - A short thank-you from the couple to express gratitude to attendees.
    - **Food:** Opt for comfort food, family-style meals, or a casual buffet to keep the atmosphere light.
3. **Etiquette Do's and Don'ts:**
    - **Do:** Send invitations early, especially if it's a more formal event.
    - **Do:** Keep the timeline short to allow everyone to rest before the big day.
    - **Don't:** Overshadow the wedding day—this event should complement, not compete with, the main celebration.

Final Tip: Keep It Fun and Personal

Pre-wedding events are about celebrating your journey to the altar. Whether you keep it small and simple or go all out, focus on moments that reflect your personality and allow you to connect with the people who mean the most to you.

Travel and Accommodations

Travel and lodging are key elements of wedding planning, especially if you're hosting guests from out of town or planning your honeymoon. Ensuring your guests are comfortable and well-informed while organizing your own travel plans will help everything run smoothly. Here's how to handle it all with ease.

Ensuring Guest Comfort with Lodging and Transportation

1. **Lodging for Guests**
   - **Reserve Room Blocks:**
     - Partner with local hotels to reserve blocks of rooms at a discounted rate.
     - Aim for 2–3 options at different price points to accommodate various budgets.
   - **Proximity to Venue:**
     - Choose hotels near your wedding venue to minimize guest travel time.
     - Provide alternatives for guests who prefer Airbnb or vacation rentals.
   - **Share Information:**
     - Include lodging details on your wedding website, invitations, or save-the-dates.
     - Provide booking deadlines to ensure guests don't miss the discount.
2. **Transportation**
   - **Shuttle Services:**
     - Arrange shuttle buses or vans to transport guests between the hotel and the venue.
     - Consider multiple pickup and drop-off times for convenience.
   - **Ridesharing:**
     - Share details about ridesharing services (e.g., Uber, Lyft) in the area, including estimated costs.
     - Provide a designated drop-off and pickup point for easy navigation.
   - **Parking Options:**
     - If guests are driving, include parking details such as availability, cost, and directions.
     - Arrange valet services or reserve parking spots if possible.
3. **Welcoming Guests:**
   - Create welcome bags with essentials like water, snacks, local maps, and an itinerary for the wedding weekend.
   - Include personal touches like a thank-you note or local souvenirs to make guests feel appreciated.

Managing Your Own Travel Plans for the Honeymoon

1. **Booking Travel**
   - **Timing:**
     - Book your honeymoon at least 4–6 months in advance to secure the best deals.
     - If traveling internationally, ensure your passport is valid and check for visa requirements.
   - **Flights and Accommodations:**
     - Use travel apps or services like Hopper, Expedia, or Kayak to track flight prices.
     - Consider honeymoon packages or all-inclusive resorts to simplify planning.
   - **Travel Insurance:**

- Protect your investment with travel insurance that covers cancellations, delays, or medical emergencies.
2. **Packing Essentials**
    - **Documents:**
        - Bring copies of important documents, including passports, travel itineraries, and confirmations.
    - **Must-Haves:**
        - Don't forget sunscreen, adapters for international outlets, and comfortable clothing for your destination.
        - Pack any wedding-related keepsakes (e.g., cards or gifts) carefully if you're bringing them along.
3. **Set Expectations:**
    - If you're leaving immediately after the wedding, plan a low-key day before travel to recover and prepare.
    - If you're delaying your honeymoon, block out some post-wedding downtime to relax before returning to daily life.

Final Tip: Communication is Key

Ensure all travel details are communicated clearly to your guests and vendors to avoid confusion. Whether it's shuttle schedules or honeymoon itineraries, well-organized plans will make your wedding day and post-wedding experience seamless and stress-free.

Post-Wedding Checklist

The wedding may be over, but there are still a few important tasks to complete to wrap up the experience. From writing thank-you notes to preserving your dress and reliving memories through photos and videos, this section will help you navigate the post-wedding phase with ease.

Writing Thank-You Notes and Handling Gifts

1. **Thank-You Notes**
    - **Start Early:** Begin writing thank-you notes as soon as possible, ideally within 1–3 months of the wedding.
    - **Personalize Each Note:** Mention the specific gift or gesture and how it will be used or appreciated. For example:

- "Thank you so much for the beautiful set of wine glasses. We've already used them for our first dinner as newlyweds and will think of you every time we toast!"
    - **Divide the Work:** If both partners are writing notes, divide the guest list evenly to make the process faster and more manageable.
2. **Organizing and Storing Gifts**
    - **Keep Track:** Use a gift tracker to record who gave what, making it easier to write thank-you notes and follow up.
    - **Returns or Exchanges:** Handle any returns or exchanges promptly and check store policies for deadlines.
    - **Cash and Gift Cards:** Store monetary gifts and gift cards in a safe place until you're ready to use them. Consider allocating these funds for your honeymoon, new home, or future expenses.

Preserving Your Dress and Reliving Memories

1. **Preserving Your Dress**
    - **Professional Cleaning:**
        - Have your dress professionally cleaned as soon as possible to prevent stains from setting.
        - Look for a cleaner that specializes in wedding gown preservation.
    - **Storage Options:**
        - If you plan to keep your dress, invest in proper preservation packaging, such as an acid-free storage box or garment bag.
        - Store it in a cool, dry place away from direct sunlight and humidity.
    - **Repurposing Ideas:**
        - If you don't want to keep your dress, consider repurposing it into a cocktail dress, donating it to a charity, or using it to create keepsakes like a christening gown or quilt.
2. **Reliving Memories Through Photos and Videos**
    - **Photo Delivery Timeline:**
        - Most photographers deliver photos within 4–8 weeks. Confirm this timeline in advance.
    - **Creating Albums:**
        - Work with your photographer to design a professional album, or use online tools like Shutterfly or Mixbook to create your own.
    - **Video Highlights:**
        - For videography, expect a timeline of 6–12 weeks for your final wedding video. Many videographers provide highlight reels or full-length edits.
    - **Share the Memories:**

- Share select photos and video clips with friends and family on social media or a wedding website.
- Consider hosting a small gathering with close family to view the wedding video together.

Final Tip: Reflect and Enjoy

Take time to reflect on your wedding day and enjoy the memories you've created. Whether it's flipping through your photo album, rewatching your wedding video, or cherishing thank-you notes from guests, these moments will remind you of the love and joy you shared on your special day.

Conclusion: Enjoy Your Special Day

Your wedding day is finally here—the culmination of all your planning, effort, and love. It's a day to celebrate your commitment and the beginning of a new chapter in your life. While it's natural to feel a mix of emotions, remember that the most important thing is to enjoy every moment.

Encouragement to Relax and Cherish the Big Day

- **Let Go of Perfection:** No wedding goes exactly as planned, and that's part of its charm. The unexpected moments—whether it's a misplaced detail or an unscripted laugh—often become the most cherished memories.
- **Trust Your Team:** Your vendors, friends, and family are there to support you. Lean on them and let them handle the logistics while you focus on soaking in the day.
- **Celebrate Your Love:** This is the one day in your life where everyone you love has gathered to celebrate you and your partner. Let that joy and love surround you and carry you through the day.

Tips for Staying Present and Enjoying the Moment

1. **Pause and Take It All In:**
    - Take a few quiet moments with your partner to step back and observe the celebration. Look around at the faces of your loved ones and the life you're building together.
2. **Don't Rush:**
    - Allow yourself to slow down and savor each part of the day. Whether it's the walk down the aisle, your first dance, or cutting the cake, be mindful and present in each moment.
3. **Focus on What Matters:**

- Don't sweat the small stuff. The flowers, the timeline, or the weather won't matter nearly as much as the love and happiness you'll feel.
4. **Spend Time with Guests:**
    - Make an effort to greet and thank your guests. A quick hug or a shared laugh can make both you and your guests feel more connected to the celebration.
5. **Enjoy the Celebration:**
    - Dance, laugh, eat, and fully immerse yourself in the joy of the day. This is a once-in-a-lifetime experience—embrace it wholeheartedly.

Your Story Begins Here

Your wedding is the start of something extraordinary. Whether it's a grand celebration or an intimate gathering, the memories you create today will last a lifetime. Relax, be present, and enjoy this special day—it's yours to cherish.

Congratulations and best wishes as you begin this beautiful journey together!

Additional Resources

Planning a wedding can feel overwhelming, but the right tools can make the process easier. Below, you'll find practical resources to help you stay organized, track expenses, and ensure no detail gets overlooked. These sample budgets, timelines, and checklists are designed to adapt to weddings of all sizes and styles.

Sample Budgets

A breakdown of common wedding expenses to help you allocate your funds:

Example Budget for a $20,000 Wedding

- **Venue and Catering:** $10,000 (50%)
- **Photography and Videography:** $3,000 (15%)
- **Attire (Dress, Suit, Accessories):** $2,000 (10%)
- **Florals and Decor:** $1,500 (7.5%)
- **Music/Entertainment:** $1,500 (7.5%)
- **Stationery (Invitations, Save-the-Dates):** $500 (2.5%)
- **Wedding Planner:** $1,000 (5%)
- **Miscellaneous (Favors, Transportation):** $500 (2.5%)

Tips:

- Adjust percentages based on your priorities. For example, if photography is a must-have for you, shift more of your budget there.
- Keep a contingency fund (5–10% of your total budget) for unexpected expenses.

Sample Day-of Timeline

For a 4:00 PM Ceremony

- **8:00 AM – 10:00 AM:** Hair and makeup for the bridal party.
- **10:00 AM – 12:00 PM:** Bride finishes hair and makeup; groom gets ready.
- **12:00 PM – 1:30 PM:** First look and couple's portrait.
- **1:30 PM – 3:00 PM:** Wedding party and family photos.
- **3:00 PM – 3:30 PM:** Guests begin arriving at the venue.
- **4:00 PM – 4:30 PM:** Ceremony.
- **4:30 PM – 5:30 PM:** Cocktail hour; couple and family take final portraits with guests if needed.

- **5:30 PM – 10:00 PM:** Reception with dinner, toasts, dances, and other activities.
- **10:00 PM:** Grand exit and send-off.

Essential Checklists

1. **Wedding Planning Checklist**
    - **12–18 Months Before:**
        - Set a budget.
        - Create a guest list.
        - Book the venue.
        - Hire key vendors (photographer, caterer, planner).
    - **6–12 Months Before:**
        - Send save-the-dates.
        - Shop for attire.
        - Finalize decor and floral arrangements.
    - **1–6 Months Before:**
        - Send invitations.
        - Create a seating chart.
        - Confirm vendor details.
    - **1–4 Weeks Before:**
        - Final dress fitting.
        - Prepare a day-of timeline.
        - Pack a wedding day emergency kit.
2. **Day-of Essentials Checklist**
    - Rings.
    - Marriage license.
    - Vows (if written).
    - Timeline copies for vendors and the wedding party.
    - Emergency kit: safety pins, stain remover, tissues, pain reliever, etc.

These tools will help you stay on track and ensure that all your wedding details come together seamlessly.

Vendor Interview Templates

When hiring wedding vendors, asking the right questions can help you find professionals who align with your vision, style, and budget. Below are templates for interviewing key vendors, including caterers, photographers, florists, and DJs. Customize these based on your needs and priorities.

---

1. Photographer/Videographer Interview Template

- **Experience and Style:**
    - How many weddings have you photographed/filmed?
    - How would you describe your style (traditional, photojournalistic, artistic, cinematic)?
    - Can you provide a full gallery or video from a recent wedding?
- **Availability and Team:**
    - Are you available on my wedding date?
    - Will you personally shoot/film the wedding, or will it be an associate?
    - Do you bring a second shooter or assistant?
- **Logistics and Deliverables:**
    - How many hours of coverage are included in your packages?
    - What's the turnaround time for photos/videos?
    - How do you deliver the final product (USB, online gallery, prints)?
- **Pricing and Contract Details:**
    - What are your package options, and what's included?
    - Are there additional fees (travel, overtime, etc.)?
    - What's your cancellation and refund policy?

---

2. Caterer Interview Template

- **Experience and Menu Options:**
    - Have you catered weddings at my venue before?
    - Do you offer menu tastings, and is there a fee?
    - Can you accommodate dietary restrictions (vegetarian, gluten-free, allergies)?
- **Service Style and Logistics:**
    - What service styles do you offer (plated, buffet, family-style)?
    - How do you handle set-up, serving, and cleanup?
    - Do you provide tableware, linens, and glassware?
- **Pricing and Contract Details:**
    - What's the price per person, and what's included?

- Are gratuities, service fees, or delivery fees included?
- What's your cancellation policy, and are deposits refundable?

---

3. Florist Interview Template

- **Experience and Design:**
    - Can you show examples of weddings you've designed?
    - Have you worked at my venue before?
    - What's your process for creating a cohesive floral design?
- **Flowers and Arrangements:**
    - Can you work with my color palette and theme?
    - What seasonal flowers do you recommend for my wedding date?
    - Do you provide additional decor (candles, vases, archways)?
- **Pricing and Delivery:**
    - How do you price your services (per arrangement, overall package)?
    - Are setup and breakdown included in the price?
    - What's your policy on substitutions if specific flowers are unavailable?

---

4. DJ/Band Interview Template

- **Experience and Style:**
    - Have you performed at weddings before?
    - Can you share recordings or videos of past performances?
    - How do you handle song requests and create playlists?
- **Equipment and Logistics:**
    - Do you bring your own sound system and microphones?
    - Do you provide lighting effects or additional equipment?
    - How much time do you need for setup and breakdown?
- **Pricing and Timeline:**
    - What's included in your package (hours of performance, emceeing)?
    - What's your overtime rate if the reception runs late?
    - Do you have a backup plan in case of equipment failure or emergencies?

---

5. Wedding Planner Interview Template

- **Experience and Specialties:**
  - How many weddings have you planned?
  - What's your approach to managing timelines and vendors?
  - Do you specialize in any particular styles or themes?
- **Services and Packages:**
  - What's included in your planning packages (full-service, partial, day-of coordination)?
  - How often will we meet, and how do you prefer to communicate?
  - Will you attend vendor meetings and walkthroughs with us?
- **Pricing and Contract Details:**
  - What are your fees, and how is payment structured?
  - Are travel or additional meeting fees included?
  - What's your cancellation policy?

Tips for Vendor Interviews

- **Be Prepared:** Bring a notebook or use a digital tracker to record their answers.
- **Ask for References:** A great vendor will happily provide reviews or client references.
- **Follow Your Gut:** Beyond the answers, assess their professionalism, enthusiasm, and how well they understand your vision.

Wedding Planning Apps and Websites

Here's a curated list of helpful wedding planning apps and websites to streamline your planning process. From managing budgets and timelines to finding inspiration and connecting with vendors, these tools will keep you organized and on track.

Comprehensive Wedding Planning Platforms

1. **The Knot**
   - **What It Offers:** Wedding website builder, guest list manager, budget tracker, and vendor directory.
   - **Website:** theknot.com
   - **App:** Available on iOS and Android.
2. **WeddingWire**
   - **What It Offers:** Vendor reviews, seating chart tools, budget tracker, and inspiration galleries.
   - **Website:** weddingwire.com
   - **App:** Available on iOS and Android.

3. **Zola**
    - **What It Offers:** Wedding registry, free wedding websites, guest list manager, and a planning checklist.
    - **Website:** zola.com
    - **App:** Available on iOS and Android.

Budgeting and Guest Management

4. **Joy**
    - **What It Offers:** All-in-one wedding planner with guest list manager, RSVP tracking, and photo sharing.
    - **Website:** withjoy.com
    - **App:** Available on iOS and Android.
5. **Honeyfund**
    - **What It Offers:** Honeymoon and cash gift registry, allowing guests to contribute to experiences instead of traditional gifts.
    - **Website:** honeyfund.com

Inspiration and Design

6. **Pinterest**
    - **What It Offers:** Endless inspiration for decor, dresses, themes, and DIY ideas. Create boards to organize your vision.
    - **Website:** pinterest.com
    - **App:** Available on iOS and Android.
7. **Style Me Pretty**
    - **What It Offers:** Curated inspiration for luxury and unique weddings, including real wedding features and vendor recommendations.
    - **Website:** stylemepretty.com

Vendor Search

8. **Thumbtack**
    - **What It Offers:** Find and hire local vendors, from photographers to florists, based on reviews and quotes.

- **Website:** thumbtack.com
- **App:** Available on iOS and Android.

NOTE: When you contact a vendor through platforms like Thumbtack, vendors are charged a fee—even if you don't hire them. For instance, I personally pay Thumbtack and Google anywhere from $500 to $1,500 on average for each booking I receive, and even just a contact can cost up to $150. About 50% of the leads vendors receive on those two are spam, which Google and Thumbtack do not refund and will still bill that vendor. Because of these high marketing costs, many vendors are forced to increase their prices to cover expenses.

I recommend only reaching out to vendors on Thumbtack or Bark if you're seriously considering hiring them. If you just want to ask questions or learn more, visit their website and contact them directly, and avoid using Thumbtack at all if possible. For example, on my website, **VIDART.org**, I have a live chat feature specifically for answering questions, and a phone, contact form and email. Taking this extra step can help keep costs down for vendors, which in turn helps them maintain competitive pricing for clients. If you are having trouble finding a photographer on Google, look up your state's professional photographer association, they will have a list of all photographers local to your area and their websites.

9. **Bark**
    - **What It Offers:** A platform for finding professionals, including DJs, photographers, and planners, with price estimates and reviews.
    - **Website:** bark.com

Task Management and Collaboration

10. **Trello**
- **What It Offers:** Customizable boards to track tasks, deadlines, and ideas collaboratively with your partner or wedding party.
- **Website:** trello.com
- **App:** Available on iOS and Android.
11. **Todoist**
- **What It Offers:** Task management app with reminders and shared lists to keep track of deadlines and details.
- **Website:** todoist.com
- **App:** Available on iOS and Android.

DIY Tools and Printables

12. **Canva**
    - **What It Offers:** Easy-to-use design tool for creating invitations, programs, signage, and thank-you cards.
    - **Website:** canva.com
    - **App:** Available on iOS and Android.
13. **Minted**
    - **What It Offers:** Beautifully designed, customizable stationery, including invitations, save-the-dates, and wedding programs.
    - **Website:** minted.com

Final Tip

Bookmark or download a few of these apps to get started, and choose the ones that best fit your needs and style. These tools are designed to reduce stress and give you more time to enjoy the planning process.

DIY Wedding Photography, Videography, Catering, DJ, and More

Planning a wedding on a tight budget or looking to add a personal touch to your special day? Doing some of the work yourself or enlisting help from friends and family can save money and create memorable, unique experiences. Here's a guide to DIYing major wedding elements effectively.

DIY Wedding Photography

1. **Equipment:**
    - Use a DSLR camera, mirrorless camera, or even a smartphone with a high-resolution camera.
    - Rent affordable photography equipment like lenses, lighting, and tripods if needed. But it DIY, it's best to work with what you have and only rent what you need. Expensive cameras only help those who know how to use them; if the person handling them has no experience, consider a smartphone or a cheaper camera that automates the focus and exposure.
2. **Tips:**
    - **Assign a Photographer:** Enlist a talented friend or family member who enjoys photography.
    - **Plan the Shot List:** Provide them with a checklist of must-have moments (e.g., first kiss, cake cutting, group photos).
    - **Use Natural Light:** Outdoor weddings and venues with large windows make it easier to get great shots without professional lighting.
    - **Use a Tripod:** For group shots and steady images.

- **Editing Tools:** Free or low-cost software like Lightroom Mobile, Snapseed, or Canva can help polish your photos.

DIY Wedding Videography

1. **Equipment:**
   - Use smartphones with stabilizers or rent affordable video cameras.
   - A gimbal or tripod will stabilize shots for a professional look.
2. **Tips:**
   - **Delegate Tasks:** Assign friends to capture different angles during key moments (e.g., vows, first dance).
   - **Pre-Record Messages:** Have guests record messages or toasts for a personal touch.
   - **Editing Tools:** Free software like iMovie (Mac) or DaVinci Resolve (PC) can create professional-looking videos.
   - **Batteries and Memory:** Make sure you have enough battery life, or spare batteries, and memory or SD cards, to record the footage. Make sure you're filming at least in 720p HD for the resolution, 1080p and 4k resolutions are preferred but can drain batteries and memory cards more quickly though. Make sure the person managing the camera checks the batteries and memory and changes them before important moments so the camera does not go dead during a critical moment. Autofocus on cameras is often not very good; but if they have a cheaper camera or smartphone using a wide lens, the depth of field should be wide enough that you won't have to worry about issues such as the bride or groom being out of focus.

DIY Wedding Catering

1. **Plan a Simple Menu:**
   - Focus on dishes that are easy to prepare in advance, like pasta, salads, sandwiches, or BBQ.
   - Choose foods that don't require heating on-site, such as charcuterie boards or cold appetizers.
2. **Enlist Helpers:**
   - Ask friends or family with cooking experience to help prepare dishes.
   - Hire a few servers to manage plating, serving, and cleanup if needed.
3. **Rent Equipment:**
   - Look for rental companies that provide chafing dishes, serving trays, and utensils.
   - If hosting outdoors, consider renting portable coolers or grills.
4. **DIY Beverage Station:**
   - Set up a self-serve drink station with wine, beer, and signature cocktails.
   - Add dispensers for water, lemonade, and iced tea for non-alcoholic options.

DIY Wedding DJ or Music

1. **Equipment:**
    - Rent a basic sound system with speakers, a mixer, and a microphone, or buy a speaker and hook it up to your phone using bluetooth.
    - Use a laptop, tablet, or smartphone to play music.
2. **Create a Playlist:**
    - Use Spotify or Apple Music to build a wedding playlist with different sections (e.g., pre-ceremony, reception, dance floor).
    - Include popular crowd-pleasers and slow songs for variety.
3. **Appoint an MC:**
    - Ask a friend to manage the playlist, make announcements, and keep the event flowing.
4. **Add Fun Elements:**
    - Use apps like VirtualDJ or DJay to mix songs and create seamless transitions.
    - Add karaoke for some late-night entertainment!

DIY Wedding Decor

1. **Flowers:**
    - Buy flowers in bulk from a local market or online wholesalers like Costco or FiftyFlowers.
    - Arrange bouquets, centerpieces, and boutonnieres yourself or with friends.
2. **Table Settings:**
    - Use simple, elegant items like mason jars, tea lights, or eucalyptus garlands for centerpieces.
    - Thrift or rent tableware for a charming, eclectic look.
3. **Signage and Backdrops:**
    - Design custom signs for seating charts, welcome messages, or menus using Canva or Etsy templates.
    - Create photo backdrops with fairy lights, fabric drapes, or greenery.

DIY Wedding Cake and Desserts

1. **Simple Cakes:**
    - Bake a simple, tiered cake or opt for cupcakes, donuts, or a dessert bar.
    - Use cake toppers and fresh flowers for decoration.
2. **Alternatives:**

- Consider a cookie table, pie station, or ice cream bar if baking isn't your forte.

Final Tips for a Successful DIY Wedding

1. **Start Early:** Give yourself plenty of time to practice and perfect your DIY projects.
2. **Ask for Help:** Don't try to do everything alone—delegate tasks to trusted friends and family.
3. **Keep It Simple:** Focus on what matters most and skip unnecessary extras.
4. **Plan Backup Options:** Have contingency plans in place for things like weather, technology issues, or last-minute changes.

Wedding Poses for Stylized Wedding Portraits

Here's a comprehensive list of poses to guide couples and photographers when creating stylized and memorable wedding portraits. These poses can be tailored to suit different settings, themes, and personalities.

Classic and Timeless Poses

1. **The Traditional Portrait**
    - The couple stands side-by-side, holding hands, with soft smiles.
    - Perfect for formal and classic shots.
2. **The Forehead Touch**
    - The couple leans in, gently touching foreheads while closing their eyes.
    - Creates an intimate and romantic vibe.
3. **The Embrace**
    - One partner wraps their arms around the other's waist while facing the camera.
    - Alternate: One looks at the camera while the other looks lovingly at their partner.
4. **The Side Hug**
    - The couple stands close, with one arm around each other's waist and the other free, slightly angled toward the camera.

Romantic Poses

5. **The Lift**
    - The groom (or stronger partner) lifts the bride (or other partner) off the ground while looking at each other or laughing.
6. **The Veil Shot**

- The couple shares a kiss or soft gaze under the bride's veil, creating a dreamy, ethereal effect.

7. **The Whisper**
   - One partner whispers something sweet or funny in the other's ear, capturing genuine smiles or laughter.
8. **The Hand Kiss**
   - One partner gently kisses the other's hand while the other looks down with a soft smile.

Fun and Playful Poses

9. **The Dip**
   - One partner dips the other backward, with playful expressions or a kiss.
10. **Walking Hand-in-Hand**
    - The couple walks naturally, holding hands, and looking at each other or the camera.
    - Add movement by incorporating flowing dress or veil shots.
11. **The Spin**
    - One partner twirls the other in a playful dance move, creating motion in the dress or outfit.
12. **Back-to-Back**
    - The couple stands back-to-back with arms crossed or playful expressions.

Candid Poses

13. **The Laughing Shot**
    - Capture the couple laughing together, whether from a joke or shared moment.
14. **The Sneak Peek**
    - One partner sneaks a peek at the other while they're looking in another direction, creating a candid feel.
15. **The "Stolen" Kiss**
    - Capture a kiss mid-motion, such as during a walk or after the ceremony.
16. **The Private Moment**
    - The couple leans in close, sharing a quiet, personal exchange away from the camera's direct focus.

Dramatic and Stylized Poses

17. **The Silhouette**

- Use dramatic backlighting during sunset or in a darkened space to create a striking silhouette of the couple.
18. **The Close-Up**
    - Focus on the couple's hands intertwined, rings, or a gentle touch, leaving the rest blurred.
19. **The Stairs Pose**
    - The couple stands on a grand staircase, with the bride (or partner) slightly higher to emphasize the dress/train.
20. **The Over-the-Shoulder Look**
    - One partner looks back over their shoulder at the camera while the other admires them.

Group and Wedding Party Poses

21. **Surrounded by the Wedding Party**
    - The couple in the center, with the wedding party cheering or striking fun poses around them.
22. **The Fun Wedding Party Pose**
    - Incorporate props or playful actions, like jumping or exaggerated movements.
23. **The Candid Group Shot**
    - Capture natural interaction between the couple and their party, like laughing, clinking glasses, or walking together.

Nature-Inspired Poses

24. **Under the Arch**
    - Pose beneath a floral or decorative arch, with the couple holding hands or sharing a kiss.
25. **The Meadow Walk**
    - The couple walks hand-in-hand through a field or garden, surrounded by natural beauty.
26. **The Reflection Shot**
    - Use water or mirrors to capture reflections of the couple, creating an artistic effect.
27. **The Tree Pose**
    - Incorporate a large tree as a backdrop, with the couple leaning against it or holding hands around the trunk.

Creative and Unique Poses

28. **The Frame Pose**

- Use an actual frame, window, or archway to frame the couple creatively.
29. **The Overhead Shot**
    - Capture the couple lying on the ground, facing each other, surrounded by flowers, a veil, or decor.
30. **The Shadow Shot**
    - Highlight the couple's shadows on the ground or a wall for an abstract, artistic look.

Tips for Great Portraits

- **Communicate:** Discuss poses with your photographer to align with your vision.
- **Be Natural:** The best poses come from relaxed, natural interaction. Don't overthink it!
- **Practice:** Spend time practicing a few poses before the wedding day to feel confident.
- **Incorporate Movement:** Add motion like walking, spinning, or flowing fabric for dynamic shots.
- **Use Props:** Consider items like bouquets, umbrellas, champagne glasses, or even a pet for fun and meaningful touches.

Tips to Look Your Best in Wedding Photos

Wedding photos are some of the most cherished keepsakes of your special day. Here are practical tips to help you look and feel your best in front of the camera:

---

1. Prepare Ahead of Time

- **Hydrate:** Start drinking plenty of water a few days before the wedding to keep your skin glowing.
- **Skincare Routine:** Stick to your usual routine and avoid trying new products close to the wedding day to prevent breakouts or irritation.
- **Sleep Well:** Get a good night's sleep before the wedding to reduce puffiness and under-eye circles.

---

2. Choose the Right Makeup and Hair

- **Test It Out:** Schedule a trial run with your makeup artist and hairstylist to ensure the look suits you and photographs well.
- **Use Matte Makeup:** Shiny or dewy products can look oily under flash photography, so opt for a matte finish.
- **Highlight Naturally:** Focus on highlighting your best features—eyes, cheekbones, or lips—without overdoing it.

- **Touch-Up Kit:** Keep blotting papers, lipstick, and powder on hand for quick touch-ups throughout the day.

3. Dress for Confidence

- **Well-Fitted Attire:** Ensure your wedding dress, suit, or outfit is properly tailored. Ill-fitting clothes can make you feel uncomfortable and appear less polished in photos.
- **Comfortable Shoes:** Break in your shoes ahead of time to avoid discomfort or awkward postures.
- **Practice Walking and Posing:** Get comfortable moving and standing in your wedding attire, especially if your dress has a long train or intricate details.

4. Pose Naturally

- **Relax Your Shoulders:** Keep your shoulders relaxed to avoid stiffness.
- **Stand Tall:** Maintain good posture by pulling your shoulders back and keeping your chin slightly lifted.
- **Angle Your Body:** Stand slightly angled to the camera instead of facing it head-on. This creates a more flattering silhouette.
- **Hands Placement:** Avoid letting your arms hang awkwardly. Place your hands on your partner, hold your bouquet, or lightly touch your waist.

5. Smile Comfortably

- **Practice Smiling:** Find a natural smile that doesn't feel forced by practicing in front of a mirror.
- **Think Happy Thoughts:** Focus on your joy and excitement to create an authentic expression.
- **Soft Eyes:** Avoid a wide-eyed look by keeping your gaze relaxed and natural.

6. Use the Light to Your Advantage

- **Face the Light:** Position yourself so that natural light hits your face directly or at an angle for a soft, flattering glow.
- **Golden Hour:** Schedule portraits during the golden hour (the hour after sunrise or before sunset) for warm, beautiful lighting.

- **Avoid Harsh Shadows:** For outdoor photos, stand in shaded areas to avoid unflattering shadows on your face.

7. Focus on Your Connection

- **Interact Naturally:** Laugh, talk, or share a quiet moment with your partner to create genuine, candid expressions.
- **Look at Each Other:** Instead of always looking at the camera, focus on your partner to capture romantic moments.
- **Stay in the Moment:** Forget about the camera and enjoy the day—it's your emotions that make the photos truly special.

8. Avoid Common Pitfalls

- **Don't Over-Pose:** Be mindful of overly exaggerated poses that can feel unnatural or stiff.
- **Check Details:** Ensure your dress, veil, and hair are properly arranged before each shot.
- **Mind Your Chin:** Keep your chin slightly down to avoid a double chin, but not so far that you lose eye contact with the camera.

9. Use Props Thoughtfully

- **Bouquets:** Hold your bouquet at hip level to avoid blocking your torso.
- **Veils:** Use your veil creatively for dramatic, romantic shots.
- **Interactive Props:** Consider champagne glasses, sparklers, or meaningful items that add personality to your photos.

10. Stay Relaxed and Confident

- **Take Breaks:** If you feel overwhelmed, pause and take a few deep breaths.
- **Communicate with Your Photographer:** Share your preferences, concerns, or insecurities with your photographer so they can guide you.
- **Focus on Confidence:** The more comfortable and happy you feel, the better your photos will look.

Tips for Working with Your Photographer to Get the Best Shots

Building a strong rapport with your photographer and collaborating effectively can make a huge difference in the quality and feel of your wedding photos. Here's how to ensure you and your photographer are on the same page for stunning results:

1. Communicate Your Vision

- **Share Examples:** Show your photographer examples of styles or specific photos you love (e.g., Pinterest boards, Instagram posts).
- **Discuss Preferences:** Be clear about the mood you want—romantic, candid, fun, editorial, or a mix of styles.
- **Highlight Must-Haves:** Provide a list of essential shots, such as specific family combinations, detail shots, or unique moments like a first look.

2. Build a Relationship

- **Schedule an Engagement Shoot:** This allows you to get comfortable with your photographer and their style before the wedding day.
- **Ask Questions:** Discuss their approach to directing, posing, and capturing candid moments.
- **Trust Their Expertise:** Give your photographer creative freedom to capture unexpected moments and angles—they've done this before!

3. Plan Your Wedding Day Timeline Together

- **Allocate Enough Time:** Work with your photographer to set aside sufficient time for each part of the day, including:
  - Getting ready photos: 1–2 hours.
  - Couple's portraits: 45 minutes–1 hour.
  - Wedding party and family portraits: 30–45 minutes.
- **Golden Hour Photos:** Schedule portraits during the golden hour (just after sunrise or before sunset) for stunning, soft lighting.
- **Share the Schedule:** Make sure the photographer has your day-of timeline and knows the flow of events.

4. Choose the Right Locations

- **Scout the Venue:** Walk through the venue with your photographer before the wedding to identify ideal spots for photos.
- **Discuss Backup Plans:** For outdoor ceremonies, talk about indoor options in case of bad weather.
- **Highlight Meaningful Spots:** Let your photographer know if there are locations that hold special significance (e.g., where you got engaged).

5. Relax During the Poses

- **Follow Their Lead:** Trust your photographer's instructions for posing and angles, even if something feels a bit awkward—they know what works best for the camera.
- **Stay Natural:** Avoid forcing smiles or rigid poses. Focus on interacting with your partner or enjoying the moment.
- **Incorporate Movement:** Simple actions like walking, spinning, or swaying add life and dynamism to photos.

6. Prepare for Candid Moments

- **Be Present:** Forget about the camera and enjoy your day—candid photos often capture the most authentic moments.
- **Involve Your Guests:** Encourage spontaneous interactions with friends and family for lively group shots.
- **Capture Quiet Moments:** Let your photographer document private, emotional moments, like a pre-ceremony prayer or a quiet exchange with your partner.

7. Leverage Lighting and Atmosphere

- **Embrace Natural Light:** Outdoor photos in natural light are often the most flattering, so work with your photographer to maximize those opportunities.
- **Use Decor Creatively:** Incorporate your wedding decor—arches, floral arrangements, or string lights—for stunning backdrops.
- **Trust Flash Photography:** For indoor or evening shots, let your photographer use professional flash setups to avoid harsh shadows or poor lighting.

8. Prepare for Group Shots

- **Create a List:** Provide a detailed list of group photos, including family and wedding party combinations.
- **Assign a Helper:** Designate a trusted friend or family member to assist in gathering people for group shots quickly.
- **Limit Group Sizes:** Keep larger groups to fewer than 10 people to avoid chaotic or awkward compositions.

9. Focus on Details

- **Ask for Detail Shots:** Request close-ups of items like your rings, bouquet, dress, shoes, or invitations.
- **Get Ready Photos:** Include candid moments during hair, makeup, and getting dressed.
- **Venue and Decor:** Make sure your photographer captures wide-angle shots of your ceremony and reception spaces before guests arrive.

10. Review and Revisit

- **Discuss Post-Wedding Expectations:** Confirm the timeline for receiving your edited photos and how they will be delivered (e.g., digital gallery, USB).
- **Choose Your Favorites:** Set aside time to pick your favorite photos for albums and prints.
- **Provide Feedback:** Let your photographer know which photos or styles you loved the most—it helps them tailor future sessions for anniversaries or other milestones.

Bonus Tip: Trust the Process

Your photographer is there to make you look and feel amazing. Stay open to their ideas, relax, and focus on enjoying your day—it's your authentic joy and love that will shine through in every photo.

DIY DJ Playlist: Most Popular Wedding Songs

Creating a DIY playlist for your wedding? Here's a curated list of the most popular wedding songs across various categories, ensuring you cover every moment of your special day. These songs are guaranteed to keep the vibe romantic, energetic, and fun for all your guests.

1. Ceremony Songs

Elegant and emotional tracks for the ceremony's key moments.

Processional (Walking Down the Aisle):

- "A Thousand Years" – Christina Perri
- "Canon in D" – Johann Pachelbel
- "Marry Me" – Train
- "Perfect" – Ed Sheeran
- "Here Comes the Sun" – The Beatles (Instrumental Version)

Recessional (Walking Back as Newlyweds):

- "Signed, Sealed, Delivered (I'm Yours)" – Stevie Wonder
- "You Make My Dreams" – Hall & Oates
- "Can't Stop the Feeling!" – Justin Timberlake
- "This Will Be (An Everlasting Love)" – Natalie Cole
- "Happy" – Pharrell Williams

2. First Dance Songs

Romantic tracks to set the mood for your first dance as a married couple.

- "At Last" – Etta James
- "All of Me" – John Legend
- "Thinking Out Loud" – Ed Sheeran
- "You Are the Best Thing" – Ray LaMontagne
- "Speechless" – Dan + Shay
- "I Don't Want to Miss a Thing" – Aerosmith
- "Can't Help Falling in Love" – Elvis Presley (or Haley Reinhart's version)

3. Parent Dances

Heartwarming songs for parent-child dances.

Father-Daughter Dance:

- "My Girl" – The Temptations
- "Butterfly Kisses" – Bob Carlisle

- "I Loved Her First" – Heartland
- "Isn't She Lovely" – Stevie Wonder
- "Dance with My Father" – Luther Vandross

Mother-Son Dance:

- "A Song for Mama" – Boyz II Men
- "Forever Young" – Rod Stewart
- "Humble and Kind" – Tim McGraw
- "What a Wonderful World" – Louis Armstrong
- "You Raise Me Up" – Josh Groban

4. Dinner and Cocktail Hour

Smooth and light background music for mingling and dining.

- "Beyond" – Leon Bridges
- "L-O-V-E" – Nat King Cole
- "Home" – Michael Bublé
- "Come Away With Me" – Norah Jones
- "Better Together" – Jack Johnson
- "Just the Way You Are" – Billy Joel
- "How Sweet It Is (To Be Loved By You)" – James Taylor

5. Dance Floor Openers

High-energy songs to get everyone up and moving.

- "Uptown Funk" – Mark Ronson ft. Bruno Mars
- "Shut Up and Dance" – WALK THE MOON
- "I Wanna Dance with Somebody" – Whitney Houston
- "Don't Stop Believin'" – Journey
- "Dynamite" – Taio Cruz
- "Shake It Off" – Taylor Swift
- "We Found Love" – Rihanna ft. Calvin Harris

6. Party Favorites

Songs that always bring the energy and fun.

- "Yeah!" – Usher ft. Lil Jon, Ludacris
- "Mr. Brightside" – The Killers
- "Sweet Caroline" – Neil Diamond
- "Livin' on a Prayer" – Bon Jovi
- "September" – Earth, Wind & Fire
- "Party in the USA" – Miley Cyrus
- "Old Town Road" – Lil Nas X

7. Group Dances and Crowd Pleasers

Songs that bring everyone to the dance floor.

- "Cha Cha Slide" – DJ Casper
- "Cupid Shuffle" – Cupid
- "Wobble" – V.I.C.
- "Macarena" – Los Del Rio
- "Shout" – The Isley Brothers
- "Twist and Shout" – The Beatles

8. Last Dance Songs

End the night on a memorable and romantic note.

- "Closing Time" – Semisonic
- "Take Me Home, Country Roads" – John Denver
- "(I've Had) The Time of My Life" – Bill Medley & Jennifer Warnes
- "Don't Stop Me Now" – Queen
- "Bohemian Rhapsody" – Queen
- "Sweet Child O' Mine" – Guns N' Roses
- "Perfect Day" – Lou Reed

Tips for a DIY DJ Wedding Playlist

1. **Create Separate Playlists:** Organize your playlist into categories (e.g., ceremony, dinner, dancing).
2. **Test Transitions:** Use apps like Spotify or Apple Music to preview transitions between songs.
3. **Include Crowd Favorites:** Mix newer hits with classics to keep all age groups happy.
4. **Backup Your Playlist:** Bring your playlist on multiple devices (e.g., laptop, phone, or USB).
5. **Appoint a Music Manager:** Ask a friend to manage the playlist and announcements so you can focus on enjoying your day.

TOP 100 Wedding Songs

1. "I Wanna Dance with Somebody" – Whitney Houston
2. "September" – Earth, Wind & Fire
3. "Uptown Funk" – Mark Ronson ft. Bruno Mars
4. "Shut Up and Dance" – WALK THE MOON
5. "Don't Stop Believin'" – Journey
6. "Marry You" – Bruno Mars
7. "Crazy in Love" – Beyoncé ft. JAY-Z
8. "Sweet Caroline" – Neil Diamond
9. "Can't Stop the Feeling!" – Justin Timberlake
10. "Hey Ya!" – OutKast
11. "Dancing Queen" – ABBA
12. "All of Me" – John Legend
13. "Thinking Out Loud" – Ed Sheeran
14. "Signed, Sealed, Delivered (I'm Yours)" – Stevie Wonder
15. "24K Magic" – Bruno Mars
16. "We Found Love" – Rihanna ft. Calvin Harris
17. "I Gotta Feeling" – The Black Eyed Peas
18. "Livin' on a Prayer" – Bon Jovi
19. "Happy" – Pharrell Williams
20. "Billie Jean" – Michael Jackson
21. "A Thousand Years" – Christina Perri
22. "You Make My Dreams" – Daryl Hall & John Oates
23. "At Last" – Etta James
24. "Treasure" – Bruno Mars
25. "Footloose" – Kenny Loggins
26. "Brown Eyed Girl" – Van Morrison
27. "Shake It Off" – Taylor Swift
28. "Love Shack" – The B-52's
29. "You Are the Best Thing" – Ray LaMontagne
30. "Blurred Lines" – Robin Thicke ft. T.I. & Pharrell
31. "Twist and Shout" – The Beatles

32. "Superstition" – Stevie Wonder
33. "Ho Hey" – The Lumineers
34. "All You Need Is Love" – The Beatles
35. "Sugar" – Maroon 5
36. "Best Day of My Life" – American Authors
37. "Pour Some Sugar on Me" – Def Leppard
38. "Crazy Little Thing Called Love" – Queen
39. "Party Rock Anthem" – LMFAO
40. "Let's Get It On" – Marvin Gaye
41. "Stayin' Alive" – Bee Gees
42. "SexyBack" – Justin Timberlake
43. "Friends in Low Places" – Garth Brooks
44. "Yeah!" – Usher ft. Lil Jon & Ludacris
45. "Wonderful Tonight" – Eric Clapton
46. "Get Lucky" – Daft Punk ft. Pharrell Williams
47. "Rock Your Body" – Justin Timberlake
48. "Respect" – Aretha Franklin
49. "Baby Got Back" – Sir Mix-A-Lot
50. "Single Ladies (Put a Ring on It)" – Beyoncé
51. "Boogie Wonderland" – Earth, Wind & Fire with The Emotions
52. "Jump Around" – House of Pain
53. "My Girl" – The Temptations
54. "Levitating" – Dua Lipa ft. DaBaby
55. "Wobble" – V.I.C.
56. "Cupid Shuffle" – Cupid
57. "Cha Cha Slide" – DJ Casper
58. "Shallow" – Lady Gaga & Bradley Cooper
59. "Perfect" – Ed Sheeran
60. "From This Moment On" – Shania Twain & Bryan White
61. "Firework" – Katy Perry
62. "God Only Knows" – The Beach Boys
63. "Isn't She Lovely" – Stevie Wonder
64. "Higher Love" – Kygo & Whitney Houston
65. "Ain't No Mountain High Enough" – Marvin Gaye & Tammi Terrell
66. "XO" – Beyoncé
67. "Forever" – Chris Brown
68. "Your Song" – Elton John
69. "Something Just Like This" – The Chainsmokers & Coldplay
70. "Die a Happy Man" – Thomas Rhett

71. "Country Roads" – John Denver
72. "Don't Start Now" – Dua Lipa
73. "Wake Me Up" – Avicii
74. "Let's Stay Together" – Al Green
75. "First Day of My Life" – Bright Eyes
76. "Tennessee Whiskey" – Chris Stapleton
77. "Everything" – Michael Bublé
78. "Landslide" – Fleetwood Mac
79. "Say You Won't Let Go" – James Arthur
80. "Heaven" – Bryan Adams
81. "Marry Me" – Train
82. "Endless Love" – Diana Ross & Lionel Richie
83. "No Tears Left to Cry" – Ariana Grande
84. "Speechless" – Dan + Shay
85. "She Will Be Loved" – Maroon 5
86. "Can't Help Falling in Love" – Elvis Presley (or Haley Reinhart version)
87. "If I Ain't Got You" – Alicia Keys
88. "Latch" – Disclosure ft. Sam Smith
89. "Love on Top" – Beyoncé
90. "Stay With Me" – Sam Smith
91. "Time of Our Lives" – Pitbull & Ne-Yo
92. "Shake Your Body (Down to the Ground)" – The Jacksons
93. "Rock With You" – Michael Jackson
94. "How Sweet It Is (To Be Loved by You)" – James Taylor
95. "You're Still the One" – Shania Twain
96. "The Way You Look Tonight" – Frank Sinatra
97. "We Are Family" – Sister Sledge
98. "Old Town Road" – Lil Nas X ft. Billy Ray Cyrus
99. "I'll Be" – Edwin McCain
100. "Wonderful World" – Louis Armstrong

About the Author

Michael Szymczyk is an independent filmmaker, photographer, philosopher and novelist. He is the writer and director of six feature films: *Scent, Eaters of the Dead, SARS-29, Journey to the End of the Night, Night of the Skinwalkers* and *The Reality of Time*. He is also the author of *Atlantis & Its Fate In The Postdiluvian World: A Possible Site for Plato's Atlantis by Kodiak Island, Independent Filmmaking 101, Cinematography 101, German 101, French 101, Latin 101, Spanish 101, Hyperborea & The Lost Age of Man, Tristan MacArthur in the 36th Century*, and more.

Michael's first novel received notable mentions in various newspapers and he was briefly featured in *Publisher's Weekly*:

- "Another candidate for the canon?" - Mike Thomas, *Chicago Sun-Times*
- "Szymczyk is smart." - Mark Eberhardt, *The Kansas City Star*

Made in United States
Cleveland, OH
19 February 2025